BIRDS AND HUMANS: WHO ARE

David Campbell Callender

as

Professor Ruth Finnegan

CALLENDER NATURE
2022

www.ruthhfinnegan.com

Callender Press I callenderpress.co.uk I Milton Keynes

ISBN 9-781739-893781

Callender Press

Contents

Preface

David Campbell Callender (1860-1926) was a gentle Irish naturalist living in Derry who was left to manage his failing family business, yet traced the flight of birds, founded a museum, looked to the hills, and watched the grass grow beautiful under his feet.

This book is written in his honour and memory, in an affectionate account that he might himself have written and with images that he might have chosen, by his granddaughter Ruth Finnegan in July 2021.

Writing as Ruth Finnegan I should make clear, though I suppose it will be obvious, that this is a book of common parlance rather than of expert science so I have as far as possible avoided specialist terminology and Latin names. There are plenty of excellent and highly recommended books that provide full scientific information and terminology if that is what you need, this is just not one of them.

As Ruth, too, I have loved preparing this book. Of course, I have always admired birds – their colour, their bright skill, their cooperative activities and individuality, who wouldn't – but I had no idea … What amazing creatures they are! How incredibly, in parallel lives to us humans, they seem indeed to be another miracle of our beautiful earth even though their quality is not always fully appreciated. Given this and the wealth of books and knowledge about *homo sapiens*, my main though not exclusive focus has been on the *birds*. Fear not, humans are there too, and we return to them directly in the closing sections.

I hope you find something of the same joy in reading about these wonderful beings as I do in putting together this attempt to appreciate something of their elusive being.

Again, as Ruth, I write as an anthropologist with long interests in music, language, communication and comparative culture, thinking now that I would like to extend this to the culture of birds. Let me also add that in general I find it more natural to follow a practice by now long established in my own discipline of anthropology, of where possible speaking – and thinking – of individuals and groups rather than of The Conglomerate Species (once we get away from dinosaur fossils, that is). Thus, I tend to write, for example, of "swallows" or "a swallow" rather than of "The Swallow (*hirundo rustica*)" – it somehow feels more down to earth and – why not? – a touch more respectful.

Acknowledgements

This is not an academic work in the normal sense (after a lifetime in academe I do know what those are like) but a work for general reading, so have not tried to put in a reference for each point or controversy that I've touched on or to detail every single one of the sources I have used, rather I've gathered together the main sources and references at the end so that anyone who wishes to take this further or test out the account here will be able to do so. I do need to add that an over-arching work like the present inevitably relies on an immense range of sources – specialist academic articles, general books about birds, comparative literature, videos, birders' detailed reports (too many to list) – and spread across a variety of disciplines. A selection is mentioned in the References at the end, chief among them the amazingly informative articles in Wikipedia (where else for the latest expert overviews?), extensively relied on here and both directly and indirectly quoted – my most sincere thanks.

In addition, I wish to express my gratitude for the images – what would an account like this be without pictures (if I have inadvertently used any wrongly, please forgive me and get in touch).

I specially wish to thank my good friend John Hunt, cartographer and bird lover for his stunning photographs, layout and pagination, Wikipedia, NASA, and the most generous photographers in the world, those of Pixaby and particularly, of Unsplash.

Front cover: Stained glass window by Marc Chagall, Saillant Chapel, Le Saillant, Correze, Voutezac, France. The Le Saillant Chapel is the only chapel in France and one of the only four chapels in the world to have been entirely decorated with stained-glass windows by Marc Chagall (1887-1985) a Belarusian-French artist. An early modernist, he was associated with several major artistic styles and created works in a wide range of artistic formats, including painting, drawings, book illustrations, stained glass, stage sets, ceramics, tapestries and fine art prints.

Photo by: John Hunt

I remember...

I was born in the days when babies were put outside in their prams to get the air, and my first memory – I must have been only a few months – is of lying on my back looking up into the rowan tree that grew in the middle of my granny's back garden and hearing, or rather feeling, a gentle little rustling flutter in the branches above me.

I wasn't old enough to wonder what it was but I have never, even now in my 80s, lost that memory and the feeling of mystery and excitement that it brought me.

And then, later, a toddler stumbling through the park opposite my granny's house trying to catch up with her and my mother, I remember stopping to watch a little bird hopping round in the grass. On my level. Making friends. I couldn't talk to tell my mother what it was but she saw my eyes following it and I knew she and my granny were pleased too and that birds were one of the joys of life.

And then there were those childhood wanders and stoppings under the trees to the melodies of thrushes and blackbirds – I probably did not know the word "inspiration" but I think that's what it was, perhaps too the start of my lifelong love of music. Then later brisk walks with my almost too know-all birding aunt: pointing out every little flutter or edge of a feather – a bit overwhelming, but it meant I got to feel the flap of a wing, the soar, the miraculous nests and colours.

I recall too walking through the woods with my classical-scholar father as we heard the constant voices of the pigeons and he told me that they coo in the "dochmiac" rhythm, the wildest most emotional most dramatic of all the ancient Greek meters – and they were: cooo cooo coo cooo, coocoocoo kooo coo cooo, those rhythmic stirring tones that I still hear every day from the trees opposite our house.

And in the autumn, I look and listen for the double-wedged honk honk honk of the migrating wild geese.

How could I not be fascinated by birds and want to know more about them?

It was only much later as I grew to be myself a scholar that I discovered that birds were indeed the object of research and scientific investigation, giving a route not just to admire them but to learn about and – as humans always have – from these amazing creatures.

For years I've vaguely wanted to know more but it's only now that I have thought that perhaps I should try to create a book to pass on some distillation of what I have learned and felt and loved about these wonderful parallel miracles of our earth.

So this, dear reader, dear birds of the sky and the trees, is it. Forgive its deficiencies, it is the best I can do.

What are birds?

You know birds, you see them every day.

They hop visibly on our lawns, build nests in our hedges and trees, swoop over the sea, swim in ponds and rivers, fly amazing aerobatics in the sky, show us their incredible migrating navigating flocks. They sound their calls and songs through the woods, show off their colours, inform the symbolisms of our poetry. To an extent unequalled by any other untamed animals they are truly part of our everyday life.

But what are they, really?

The answers surprised me, and may surprise you too.

Let me start with the obvious things. Birds are a group of warm–blooded vertebrates within the earth's animal kingdom, making up a class (in technical terminology, the aves) characterised by feathers, toothless beaked jaws, the laying of hard-shelled eggs, a high metabolic rate, a four-chambered heart, and a strong yet lightweight skeleton adapted for flight.

They are everywhere, for, like grass, they live in all parts of the world, even the most inhospitable places.

They are incredibly varied too. They range in size, for example, from the tiny 2.2 inch hummingbird to the 9 foot 2 inch ostrich, and come in many shapes and forms, there are between ten and eleven thousand living species.

Birds have wings, that too is obvious. These have developed from forelimbs and give birds the ability to fly through the air (there are a few exceptions as further evolution has led to the loss of flight in large birds such as ostriches, emus, rheas, cassowaries, and kiwis, also penguins, and some island species). Birds' digestive and respiratory systems are uniquely adapted for flight. Several aquatic species, particularly seabirds and water fowl, have further evolved for swimming.

WHO ARE WE?

Compared to mammals?

There are several clear differences from mammals. Whereas birds have feathers, lack teeth and lay eggs, mammals have fur or hair for insulation, possess teeth and give birth to live young.

But, although birds are more closely related to reptiles than to mammals, birds and mammals do have characteristics in common. Both are warm-blooded, which means they can maintain a constant body temperature and do not need to rely on an external heat source to stay warm. This lends itself to several other commonalities, such as similar caloric requirements by weight and the ability to remain active in colder temperatures (cold-blooded animals, such as reptiles, do not have to eat as much, but they also cannot survive colder temperatures). Being warm-blooded gives birds and mammals the unique ability to live on any landmass on earth.

There are also some behavioural traits shared between birds and humans. Both tend to be more intelligent than reptiles, amphibians, or fish. Birds and humans form social groups with complex vocal inter-communication. Both usually care for their offspring for an extended period of time, as opposed to most other animals which do not offer a high level of parental care (the length of time varies from species to species, depending on the age that the young are able to take care of themselves). Female mammals feed their young by lactating, while birds feed them beak to beak.

Birds and humans also share some traits that are due not to common ancestry but to "convergent evolution", something that occurs when species that are not closely related evolve the same or similar traits due to similar evolutionary pressures.

Birds, then, are eventually reptiles – but at the same time with some physical and, as we have increasingly become aware in recent years, cultural overlaps with mammals.

How do birds behave?

To summarise, typical bird behaviour includes cooperative living, nest building, and two–parent care of the young. Birds reproduce by laying sexually fertilised eggs, usually in a nest and incubated by the parents. With most birds there is an extended period of parental care after hatching.

Birds are essentially social and cultural beings and as such, like humans, learn and pass on knowledge from generation to generation. They are also social in the sense of communicating with each other through visual signals, calls, and songs, and of participating in such behaviour as cooperative breeding and hunting, flocking, and mobbing predators. Most species are socially (but not necessarily sexually) monogamous, usually for one breeding season at a time, sometimes for years or, as we shall see, for life.

Many species of birds are economically important to us humans as food and as raw material for manufacturing. Both domesticated and undomesticated birds are good sources of eggs, meat, and feathers. Songbirds, parrots, and other species are popular as pets while guano (bird excrement) is harvested as a valuable fertiliser. In addition, birdwatching is important for study and leisure, and is now a significant part of the ecotourism industry.

In addition, for millennia and perhaps from the very ancient of times, birds have had a prominent presence in human art, music, and literature.

Finally – and this may startle you, as at first it did me – when we look at it in the context of the millions of years of evolution, birds are feathered dinosaurs, in fact the only living dinosaurs in today's world.

An illustration of *Acheroraptor temertyorum*. It's depicted staring at a hispine beetle. This bird-dinosaur has been known from teeth for many years and is named after the underworld *Acheron* of Greek mythology. Phylogenetic analysis recovers it as a *velociraptorine*, the most basal member of the group containing *Velociraptor, Adasaurus and Tsaagan*.

Where did birds come from?

Yes, believe it or not: birds are dinosaurs, the living dinosaurs of today. They have evolved and changed over many millions of years admittedly, but they are still – dinosaurs: not just *descended* from dinosaurs, they *are* dinosaurs. Just as humans belong to the scientific category of mammals, so birds belong to the scientific category of dinosaurs and their closest living relatives are crocodiles.

Look round at all those many many kinds of birds in the sky and the rocks and the trees – looking so different, can they *really,* as we now know, *be* dinosaurs? *How* could that possibly have come about? Anyway, were not the dinosaurs wiped out millions of years ago in that massive meteor impact?

Look more closely at what happened. Modern birds emerged in the Middle to Late Cretaceous era, and diversified dramatically around the time of the Cretaceous-Paleogene extinction event 66 MYA (Million Years Ago) which killed all the non-avian dinosaurs.

Then look at some of the accumulating evidence we now have of that history, both the fossils themselves and speculative projections based on the detailed fossil remains. Birds are, in summary, the descendants of primitive avialans whose members included *Archaeopteryx* who first emerged about 160 million years ago. They looked something like these (some photographed from fossil traces, some from images projected from these skeletal remains).

Fossil cast of a Sinornithosaurus millenii

Birds-evolving dinosaurs

Scientists deduce this millennia-long history from fossilised skeletons such as those pictured, supplemented by imagined but scientifically informed drawings. The gradual uncovering of the tale of bird evolution reads rather like a detective story – in fact it *is* a detective story. There was the gathering–up of the emerging shreds of evidence and counter evidence, opposing and counter-opposing theories, confusions and data that did not fit, accusations of misrepresentation, malpractice and even theft, and finally, as far as we can tell, the uncovering of the true story.

Extinct eagle birds, showing resemblance to earlier dinosaur shapes

Perhaps there was no murder – though do not forget the asteroid from space that 66 million years ago killed all the other dinosaurs. Only those to be the birds made their way and survived.

According to current research the history of birds goes something like this. It began in the Jurassic Period (201-145 million years ago), the earliest birds being derived from a form of theropod dinosaurs. These and a sister group, the order *Crocodilia*, are the sole living members of a "reptile" clade, the Archosauria.

Four lineages of bird survived the Cretaceous-Paleogene extinction event 66 million years ago: ostriches and their relatives, ducks and their relatives, ground-living fowl, and "modern birds".

Pterodactylus, literally "winged finger", was a now-extinct genus of winged dinosaurs, a step in the gradual development of birds. Fossil remains, primarily found in Bavaria, Germany, date back to the Late Jurassic period about 150.8 to 148.5 million years ago.

The pterodactyl was a generalist carnivore (meat eater) that probably fed on a variety of invertebrates and vertebrates. It had wings formed by a skin and muscle membrane stretching from its elongated fourth finger to its hind limbs. It was quite a small pterosaur compared to other famous genera and lived alongside other small pterosaurs such as the well-known *Rhamphorhynchus*. In technical terms *Pterodactylus* is classified as an early-branching member within the pterosaur clade Pterodactyloidea. Pterodactylus antiquus was the first pterosaur fossil to be identified. It was described by the Italian scientist Cosimo Alessandro Collini in 1784, based on a fossil skeleton unearthed from the Solnhofen limestone of Bavaria.

Collini was the curator of the *Naturalienkabinett* (*"nature cabinet of curiosities", precursor of the modern natural history museum). Though the actual date of the specimen's discovery is unknown it is almost certainly the earliest documented pterosaur find. General excitement!

Wagler's 1830 restoration of his speculated aquatic Pterodactylus

In his description of the specimen, Collini did not conclude that it was a flying animal. In fact, he couldn't fathom *what* kind of animal it might have been, but he ruled out any links with birds or bats. He thought it might have been a sea creature, not for any anatomical reason, but because he felt that the ocean depths were more likely to have housed unknown types of animals. The idea that pterosaurs were aquatic persisted up to 1830, when the German zoologist Johann Georg Wagler published a text on "amphibians" which included an illustration of *Pterodactylus* using its wings as flippers – an aquatic vertebrate.

The German/French scientist Johann Hermann was the one who first asserted that Pterodactylus used its long fourth finger to support a *wing* membrane.

Hermann alerted the prominent French scientist Georges Cuvier to the existence of Collini's fossil, believing that it had been captured by the occupying armies of Napoleon and sent to the French collections in Paris – something not infrequent at the time. He sent a letter with a speculative sketch showing an animal with wing membranes extending from the long fourth finger to the ankle and a (totally speculative) covering of fur.

Cuvier agreed and published these ideas in December 1800. But he added one important point. He considered that the animal was a reptile.

At this point the fossil was thought to be missing. In fact, it was with Samuel Thomas von Sömmerring, who gave a public lecture about it in December, 1810. In it he named the species Ornithocephalus antiquus, described as being a bat and something between mammals and birds. Cuvier disagreed, provided a lengthy description again claiming that it was a reptile.

It was not until 1817 that a second specimen of *Pterodactylus* came to light. This tiny

Pterodactylus antiquus

specimen was described by Von Sömmerring as *Ornithocephalus brevirostris* (named for its short snout), and a juvenile. He provided a restoration of the skeleton, the first published for any pterosaur but his sketch was in fact quite inaccurate and he did not change his belief that these creatures were bats.

This "bat model" was influential long after a consensus had been reached, around 1860, that the animals were in fact reptiles. The standard assumptions by then were that pterosaurs were quadrupedal, clumsy on the ground, furred, warm-blooded and with a wing membrane reaching the ankle (some of this has since been confirmed, some refuted, some still in dispute).

By now *Pterodactylus* (the now accepted name) is known from over 30 fossil specimens, and though most belong to juveniles, there are also some complete skeletons. Pterodactylus antiquus was a relatively small pterosaur, with an estimated adult wingspan of about 3 foot 5 inches with a crest on its skull composed mainly of soft tissues.

Pterodactylus specimens vary considerably based on age since proportions of the limb bones, size and shape of the skull, and the size and number of teeth changed as the animals grew. This led to the different growth stages being mistaken for new species of Pterodactylus, but in fact the evidence is that there is actually only one valid species of *Pterodactylus*, Pterodactylus antiquus.

What about its living and breeding patterns?

Scientists can infer a certain amount. It seems from the fossils remains that Pterodactylus antiquus bred seasonally and grew consistently during its lifetime. A new generation would have been produced seasonally and reached second-year size by the time the next generation hatched, creating distinct "clumps" of similarly-sized and aged individuals in the fossil record. This growth pattern is similar to modern crocodilians, rather than the rapid growth of modern birds.

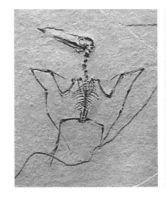

We can tell quite a lot from scleral rings, bony structures round the eyeball of many vertebrates, including birds but not humans. Vision is very important to birds for finding food, watching for predators, and judging distance for a smooth landing, so this bony ring helps by keeping their vision sharp and holding the eyeball into place. The shape and size of thus eye ring can show us what kind of lifestyle the bird had. For example, a flatter eye ring versus a tubular eye ring indicates the time of day a bird was at its most active. The scalar rings of Pterodactylus antiquus and modern birds and reptiles suggest that Pterodactylus antiquus *was* diurnal, its main activity being during the day.

As for diet: based on the shape, size, and arrangement of its teeth, Pterodactylus was a carnivore. A 2020 study of its tooth wear suggests *it* preyed mainly on small invertebrates and, indicated by a relatively high bite force, had a generalist feeding strategy.

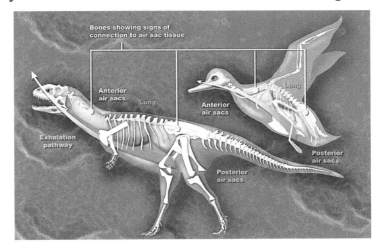

During the over 200 year history of its study, the various species of *Pterodactylus* have been classified under differing heads. In the first half of the 19th century any new pterosaur species would be named *Pterodactylus*, which thus became a "wastebasket taxon". The only well-supported species left by the first decades of the 21st century were two named P. antiquus and *P. kochi*. However, most studies between 1995 and 2010 have treated them as synonymous, the differences to be explained by differences in age (a conclusion still a little controversial but now widely accepted).

P.antiquus specimen (AMNH 1942) showing muscle impression in the chest and wing membranes

An interesting complication is that as more non-avian theropods related to birds are discovered, the formerly clear distinction between non-birds and birds becomes blurred. This had already been noted in the 19th century by Thomas Huxley:

"We have had to stretch the definition of the class of birds so as to include birds with teeth and birds with paw-like fore limbs and long tails. There is no evidence that Compsognathus possessed feathers; but, if it did, it would be hard indeed to say whether it should be called a reptilian bird or an avian reptile" (Huxley, T.H., Lectures on Evolution. New York Tribune. Extra, 1876).

Velociraptor skeleton showing the bird-like quality of the smallest theropod dinosaurs

Discoveries in northeast China demonstrated that many small theropod dinosaurs did indeed have feathers, contributing further to the ambiguity of where to draw the line between birds and reptiles. Amidst the detailed disputes however it is fairly certain that feathered wings used for flight existed in the mid-Jurassic theropods. They may not have been very good fliers, but would at least have been competent gliders, setting the stage for the evolution of full flight.

A large group of birds, the Enantiornithes, evolved in a similar way and flourished throughout the Mesozoic (about 252 to 66 million years ago), the age of the dinosaurs. Though their wings resembled those of many modern bird groups, they retained the clawed wings and a snout with teeth rather than a beak. The loss of a long tail was followed by a rapid evolution of their legs which evolved to become highly versatile and adaptable tools that opened up new ecological niches.

The Cretaceous – the final third of the Mesozoic era – saw the rise of more modern birds, now possessing a more rigid ribcage with an extension of breastbone (the keel); serving as an anchor for wing muscles, thus providing adequate leverage for flight and shoulders capable of a powerful upstroke, both essential for sustained powered flight. Another development was the appearance of a small projection (alula) on the wing edge which meant better control of landing or flight at low speeds. The general evolutionary trend has been, overall, the reduction of anatomical elements to save weight, including acquiring a light-weight skeleton.

An early example: Yanornis (fossil specimen and reconstruction)

At this stage many were coastal birds, strikingly resembling modern shorebirds or ducks. Some evolved as swimming hunters – flightless divers resembling grebes and loons. While modern in most respects, most of these birds still had typically reptilian teeth and sharp claws.

The sudden mass extinction event those 66 million years ago wiped out three-quarters of the plant and animal species on earth. The successful and dominant group of avialans, enantiornithes, perished as well. Only a small fraction of ground and water-dwelling avian species survived the impact, giving rise to today's birds. They may have been able to survive the extinction as a result of being able to dive, swim, or seek shelter in water and marshlands. Many species of avians can build burrows, or nest in tree holes, or termite nests, all of which would have provided shelter from the environmental effect. Long-term survival came as a result of filling ecological niches left empty by extinction of non–avian dinosaurs.

The general result was a sudden and very rapid diversification within this lineage (and those of other animals too), resulting eventually in the diverse, and still adapting, birds we know today.

So now – here we are. For it is to this avian lineage that almost 95% of the roughly 10,000 known species of modern birds belong.

Evolution generally occurs at a scale far too slow to be witnessed by humans. But when we reflect back on what has happened over these many ages, the story of avian evolution must seem a near incredible one. It stretches back through the mystery of eras many millions of years ago, and is still progressing.

How are they, how are we?

So now after the millions of years on this earth, not just birds but we too, we humans, are established here. We know plenty about the humans. But what of birds and their lives and cultures today? The rest of this book explores who and what *they* are, those other inhabitants of our earth: the contrasts, parallels and overlaps with humans.

Birds, it is clear, differ from humans in having a immensely longer evolutionary history. Hominids go back around 2.8 million years, long enough, but this contrasts with the 66 million or more for birds. The specific species we know as *homo sapiens* emerged only around 300,000 years ago, then, it seems, migrated out of Africa and gradually replaced local populations of other types of *hominids*.

But birds also *contrast with*, or, it might be better say complement, *homo sapiens* in certain respects which we will be exploring below. The question is: do we differ in *radical* or merely relative ways? There are several answers to this which the following chapters will pursue with the aim of elaborating and testing them. One focus will have to be on the widespread assumption that there is *a deep divide between birds* (dinosaurs, flying creatures) *and humans* (mammals). There are some obvious preliminary points. First, as well as their long evolutionary history, birds, with their many different species and subspecies, are extremely diverse compared to humans.

Then, and arguably more to the point at the present time, here, below, is list of what, though here and there a touch controversial, are generally held to be the distinctive human characteristics (in good nineteenth century-mode I have mostly added their Latin Linnaean-mode equivalents).

Two footed / two legged locomotion – homo bipedalis

A partial glimpse of the diversity of birds

This is widely seen as a key differentiating characteristic of Homo sapiens, dating back to the time when, in a crucial turning point, he (always "he" in this context) "came down" from being ape-like in the trees to walk and run – not fly – sure-footed on the ground, or (in the alternative equally credible story) "she" emerged from the sea to walk, no longer aquatic ape but now fully human, on dry land, with a two-legged gait.

Tool-using and tool-making – homo habilis et faber

This again is often seen as a criterion for being fully human, traced in plentiful archaeological discoveries of early stone tools, moving on to bronze and iron, marking the transition, as it were, into full human culture. Can any others in the animal kingdom match this?

A social being – homo socialis

Many but not all mammals are gregarious. Humans most certainly are: living essentially in groups; organising economics, politics, ritual, and play as joint ventures; sharing responsibility for parenting, scholarship, teaching, adventuring, inventing, religion. It is true that some individuals shine (or opt) out but that is assumed to be the exception within the normality of shared social existence. Humans are and presumably always have been clearly social animals.

Migrating, adventuring, navigating – homo migrans et navigans

Starting from (it now seems) South Africa, humans went out in prehistoric times to people the globe. More recently but still going back hundreds or thousands of years, they ventured in log boats, open canoes, balsa rafts to cross the oceans and inhabit new lands. In the "age of discovery" they found their way in sailing ships across the world – impressive navigation, adventuring, courage. Is there any way birds can equal this?

Speaking, planning, thinking – homo loquens et cogitans

For many – and not just Descartes' cogito ergo sum – the key thing about human beings is their capacity to think, above all to express this thought in words and be aware of their own individuality. With the largest brain of all mammals relative to their body size humans have a unique capacity for intelligence. Here surely there are no parallels among birds, are there?

Rulers of the earth – homo regnans

Though not so often stated explicitly, and despite continuing demurrals from religious circles, this is a pretty much accepted notion. That we are "the lords of creation" has been taken for granted for centuries, recently powerfully enunciated in Harari's best seller books Sapiens and Homo deus. It is we humans, no question about it it seems, who have inherited and reign over the earth – indeed by now perhaps, potentially, the universe, as we venture further year by year.

How do birds tie into all of this? There is much to investigate. We know much, from their evolutionary history, of the physical make–up of birds. But, what of their deeper inner qualities? That is what we must now turn to. For tens of thousands of years from the very start, humans have been – like birds – hunters and gatherers. Some still are, but by now agriculture is an established and necessary part of human culture. But birds? "They sow not, neither do they reap".

Locomotion

We know how we humans get around: both by the resources of our natural bodes and by mechanical means. What about the seemingly very different case of birds?

Two legs

In one way they are not so very different. A bipedal (two-footed) gait is characteristic of both birds and humans – a not uncommon form of terrestrial locomotion where an organism moves by means of its two rear limbs. All humans are bipeds, and so are birds when on the ground, a feature inherited from their dinosaur ancestors.

Types of bipedal movement include walking, running, and hopping. Relatively few modern species are habitual bipeds but among mammals, bipedalism has evolved multiple times, examples being hopping mice, pangolins and hominid apes (australopithecines and humans) as well as various extinct groups that evolved the trait independently.

A large number of modern species intermittently or briefly use a bipedal gait. Several arboreal primate species, such as gibbons and indriids, exclusively walk on two legs during the brief periods they spend on the ground. Many animals rear up on their hind legs while fighting or copulating. Some animals commonly stand on their hind legs to reach food, keep watch, threaten a competitor or predator, or pose in courtship, but do not *move* that way.

The benefit of bipedal locomotion is that it leaves the upper limbs free for manipulating things and for using and carrying tools. In birds, very different in their way of life and habitat, the free forelimbs are modified not into load carrying arms or manipulating hands but into *wings* adapted for flying, while their hind limbs are modified for walking or other bipedal movement. Their bipedalism thus spares, or invests, their forelimbs for flight.

Wings are the commonest form of avian locomotion, but moving on two feet is, for some species, an additional or, specially for the more weighty birds, sole mode of moving. Bipedal walking is in fact the normal slow gait of birds on dry land, and running the fast terrestrial gait of many of them. Birds that spend a lot of their time in trees tend to use hopping as their fast gait, and other birds to run.

Almost all birds are capable of both hopping and walking, but it is more energy efficient for small birds to hop, their light bodies easy to bounce into the air. They cover much more distance in a single hop than a walking stride from their short legs and if they spend most of their time in trees are used to hopping because they get around by jumping from branch to branch – faster and easier on narrow twigs and branches than trying to walk. These birds have evolved legs and feet that hop efficiently, so it makes sense to keep this up even when they are foraging on the ground. Each hop takes them as far as several steps would if they were walking, so they use less energy. But even though it beats walking, hopping is slower than running. Blackbirds, for example, switch from hopping to running if they are in a hurry.

Birds that nest and forage on the ground are more likely to run than to hop. This includes game birds like pheasants and grouse, but also smaller birds, such as wagtails, that chase insects on the ground. Also, for heavier more terrestrial birds, the extra load on their joints favours a gait that leaves one leg on the ground at all times. Plus, longer legs make walking faster.

Birds that forage along the seashore or estuary have often evolved long legs for wading. These allow them to cover a lot of ground efficiently with each stride. It would be quite impractical for them to hop on such spindly legs. Another shorebird, the sandpiper, runs despite its relatively short legs. This allows it to forage very close to the water's edge and still run to outstrip the incoming waves.

A few birds, like these flamingoes, even use their two legs to run on the surface of the water. Grebes too race over water in their courtship rituals, going for several yards before splashing down – an amazing spectacle (filmed at https://tinyurl.com/
p2e758m7). They generate about 50% of the force needed to stay above water by slapping their feet on the water, with all three forward-pointing toes splayed out, as fast as 20 steps per second. At the end of a stride, they retract their feet by drawing them to the side – the three front toes fold together to reduce under-water drag – before swinging them around and slapping the water again.

Though they are birds, penguins have flippers instead of wings. They cannot fly and on land they walk upright, though when snow conditions are right, they slide on their bellies. In the water they are superb swimmers, and some species can reach speeds of up to 15 miles per hour – faster than their terrestrial walking. But despite their awkward looking gait, they are expert walkers. Their yearly
migrations are famous, an astounding spectacle as they follow the tradition of generations of ancestors, travelling every year to reach their inland spots for nesting. Emperor penguins begin their migration rituals each March, travelling up to a hundred miles to reach their nesting grounds. As if by magic, penguins all across Antarctica migrate at the same time, and colonies of penguins arrive together to claim their ground. Each female lays an egg, which the males take care of for the next four months while the females trek back to the sea, where they can find food. Both parents travel the migration ways over and over for about nine months. When summer arrives and the chicks have matured, they travel with their parents to the sea and learn to swim for their own food.

Penguins may, to our eyes, only waddle but that bipedalism is essential for their way of life and, as always, the form and details of their locomotion are adapted, and effective, for the birds' needs.

Swimming

Though swimming is not the most common form of avian locomotion it is the key type of movement for water birds. Their evolution mainly centred around adaptations to improve feeding techniques, specifically legs adapted for diving or wading with webbing between the toes to aid propulsion. Webbed feet are useful on land as well as on water because they allow birds to walk more easily on mud or slimy surfaces.

Water birds are thus like other birds in using two feet for locomotion, in their case made possible through the arrangement and size of their toes. The adaptations include webbed feet, beaks, and legs adapted to move for wading, feeding in the water, and the ability to dive from the surface or the air to catch prey below the surface.

The long-webbed feet work like paddles pushing against the water and propelling the bird along. The toes fold up out of the way as each leg swings forward, just like a rower raising an oar out of the water before pushing back again with it. As the bird pulls its foot backwards through the water, the toes spread apart, letting the webs spread out and slide easily through. The foot is instantly less resistant, moving through the water easily to get into place for the next stroke without pushing the bird backwards.

Then when the bird pulls its foot forward for the next push, the toes come together, folding up the webs to propel the bird through the water.

This is a *drag-based* mode of propulsion. However, some waterfowl also use *lift-based* propulsion: their feet generate hydrodynamic lift due to the angle of attack of the foot and the relative water velocity. For example, great-crested grebes use solely lift-based propulsion due to their lateral foot stroke and asymmetric toes.

Most waterfowl use a combination of these two modes of propulsion, where the first third of their foot stroke generates propulsive drag and the last two–thirds of the stroke generates propulsive lift. During the transition from drag-based to lift-based propulsion in ducks, for instance, vortices formed on the front of the foot create a flow of water that aids lift production. The vortices from the two feet do not interfere with each other; each foot generates forward propulsion independently.

Many foot-propelled birds, including cormorants, use a combination of lift and drag during different phases of their propulsive stroke, where the often found triangular shape of bird feet allows the birds to use a similar force-generating mechanism as delta-shaped wings.

This allows for generating larger forces, and as well they rotate their feet in a way that results in lift-generated thrust. This swim style allows the birds to swim faster and more efficiently than if they used a regular paddling motion. The feet of grebes are quite special, resembling feathers, and the use of a lift-based propulsive mechanism suggests convergent evolution.

Webbed feet are a compromise between aquatic and terrestrial locomotion. The aquatic control surfaces of non-fish vertebrate can be either *paddles* or hydrofoils. Paddles generate less lift than hydrofoils, and paddling is associated with drag-based control surfaces.

Surface swimmers are speed-limited due to increasing drag as they approach a physically defined speed determined by their body length. In order to achieve speeds higher than this, eider ducks use distinctive modes of locomotion that involve lifting out of the water. They can then hydroplane, where they lift part of their body out of the water and paddle with their webbed feet to generate forces that allow them to overcome gravity; they also use paddle assisted flying, where the whole body is lifted out of the water, and the wings and feet work in concert to generate lift forces. Western and Clark's grebes utilise their lobated feet to generate nearly 50% of the force required to allow them to walk on water in elaborate sexual displays; they are likely the largest animal to "walk" on water.

Most swimming or paddling birds have legs and feet located at the rear of their body, an advantage on the water as it helps to propel the birds along. But, what's good on water isn't necessarily good on land. Having legs and feet located at the rear makes walking more difficult for these birds. However, while webbed feet have mainly arisen in the context of swimming, they can also help terrestrial movement by increasing contact area on soft surfaces.

Some birds do more than just swim. Penguins for instance also walk and slide. Those elegant swimmers, swans, can walk and fly but for them these are awkward forms of moving, and swimming is their speciality. Many duck species on the other hand are as at home on the land and in the air as in water. They possess two unique features that make them such good swimmers-webbed feet and waterproof feathers. A duck's webbed feet are specifically designed for swimming. They act as paddles, helping ducks swim fast and far, and because ducks don't have any nerves or blood vessels in their feet, they easily tolerate cold water, while their waterproof feathers keep them dry and insulate them from cold water. Like many birds, ducks have a special gland called a preen gland near their tails that produces oil. Using their bills, ducks can distribute this oil while preening to coat their feathers and provide a layer of waterproofing that keeps them slick in the water.

As well as surface feeding some seabird species *plunge* dive while foraging, the momentum counteracting buoyancy effects for a short period of time. Other species can stay submerged for longer and practise pursuit diving where they stay submerged and chase after prey with thrust from their wings, feet, or a combination of the two. Some swim extensively under the water, famous among them being penguins who glide effortlessly through the water looking as if they are flying, and expertly chase down their marine prey.

Some swimming birds rely on different propulsive mechanisms in different phases of a dive. Drag-based swimming is most often during the foraging (or bottom) phase of a dive because it provides greater manoeuvrability for pursuing prey while the more efficient lift-based swimming mechanisms are used during descent. Guillemots use lift-based swimming intermittently during the ascent phase of a dive but rely mostly on passive buoyancy forces to lift them to the surface. Swimming birds exhale before dives, reducing their air volume and thus their overall body density.

Bird anatomy is primarily adapted for efficient flight so birds that rely on swimming as well as flying have to contend with the competing requirements of flight and swimming: characteristics good in flight are detrimental to swimming. For instance, auks, who use their wings to both swim and fly, have high flight costs for their body size, and birds that use their feet to swim and are more proficient flyers have higher swim costs than wing-

Flightless Cormorant

propelled divers such as auks and penguins. The evolution of flippers in penguins was at the expense of their flying capabilities, becoming thicker, denser and smaller while being modified for hydrodynamic properties.

Bird plumage holds and deflects air which makes lift easier to achieve in flight but, again, this adaptation is detrimental to swimming because the increased air volume increases buoyancy forces. Some diving birds preen immediately before diving which expels the stored air and reduces the air volume, thus making submersion easier.

Birds that swim must also contend with the increased buoyancy effects of having lighter bones (good for flying) and a reduced body mass. Instead, diving birds increase their muscle mass, resulting in an overall increase in body mass that reduces the effects of buoyancy and makes submersion easier. This effect is predominantly seen in shallow diving birds as buoyancy effects are stronger. Faster flying speeds also result from higher wing loading which would be potentially detrimental for small flying birds who have to land precisely on small branches. Diving birds, however, do not have this constraint because open water can accommodate harder landings.

Birds that rely on lift-based propulsion for swimming may utilise higher wing beat frequencies when flying than when submerged and swimming: the increased density of water produces greater thrust for similar wing excursions, so for a given speed fewer wing beats are needed to create identical propulsion totals. Lift-based swimmers tend to have higher swim speeds and greater metabolic efficiency than drag-based swimmers because they are able to displace greater water volumes with their wings than a comparable sized bird can with its feet. Puffins both swim and fly using lift produced by their wings.

Some pursuit divers rely predominantly on their wings for thrust production during swimming. These include auks, diving petrels, and penguins. Thrust production in these animals is produced via lift principles, much like in aerial flight. These birds essentially "fly" beneath the surface of the water. Because they have the dual role of producing thrust in both flight and swimming, their wings demonstrate a compromise between the functional demands of two different fluid media.

Some birds have lost the ability to fly in favour of an aquatic lifestyle, notably penguins who are highly adapted for swimming, and flightless. Flightless cormorants have very small wings incapable of producing enough lift for flight, and swim via drag-based paddling of their webbed hind limbs.

Flying

Flying is the one of the most complex – indeed extraordinary – forms of animal movement. Well, just look!

Each facet of this type of propulsion, including hovering, taking off, and landing, involves a series of complex movements. As different bird species adapted over millions of years through evolution for specific environments, prey, predators, and other needs, they developed specialisations in their wings and their different ways of flying.

Although many birds also, as we have seen, use two-legged terrestrial and aquatic movements, *flying* is the primary mode of locomotion for most bird species. Their capacity for flight assists birds with feeding, breeding, avoiding predators, and migrating.

There are various theories about how bird flight evolved: from help in falling or gliding (the *trees down* hypothesis), from running or leaping (the *ground up* hypothesis), from *wing-assisted incline running,* or from *pouncing* actions.

Whatever the start, birds need a lot of energy to fly and avian physique has evolved to make flight easier. Unlike with mammals, bird skeletons are extremely lightweight, with *hollow* bones that manage their weight and help them to fly, but also a crisscrossed matrix for strength. The light bones allow the bird to take flight more easily, while the structural matrix adds strength to withstand the pressure of taking off and landing. This lesser body weight is highly beneficial for reducing the effects of gravity, thus making lift easier to achieve.

The strong hind limbs (legs) are also essential for taking off, landing, swimming and walking. The whole structure allows fitness and shock-absorbing during landing or take-off.

Birds also have air sacs, specialised structures closely associated with their lungs that store air when the bird inspires, further reducing body weight and maintaining the partial pressure of oxygen within the lungs equal to that of the surrounding environment.

The large amount of energy that birds need to fly necessitates a circulatory system that is both efficient and effective: a four-chambered heart with two atria and two ventricles, just like mammals. This type of circulatory system allows the separation of oxygenated and deoxygenated blood. Other species of animals, such as reptiles, have hearts with fewer chambers, which means a much less efficient model.

The most obvious adaptation to flight is the wing, but because flight is so energetically demanding birds have, as described above, evolved several other adaptations to improve efficiency when flying. As well as the hollow skeleton, birds' bodies are streamlined to help overcome air-resistance, and unnecessary bones have been lost, such as the bony tail and toothed jaw of early birds, the latter replaced with a lightweight beak. The skeleton's breastbone has also adapted into a large keel, suitable for the attachment of large, powerful flight muscles.

The feathers are also well adapted for flight. The vanes of each feather have hooklets called barbules that zip the individual feathers together, giving them the strength needed to hold the airfoil and maintaining their shape and function. Each feather has a greater side and a lesser side, meaning that the shaft does not run down its centre but longitudinally with the lesser or minor side to the front and the greater or major side to the rear of the feather. This feather anatomy during flight and flapping of the wings causes a rotation of the feather in its follicle.

The rotation occurs in the up motion of the wing. The greater side points down, letting air slip through the wing. This breaks the integrity of the wing, allowing for a much easier movement in the up direction. The integrity of the wing is re-established in the down movement, which allows for part of the lift inherent in bird wings. This function is most important in taking off or achieving lift at very low or slow speeds where the bird is reaching up and grabbing air to pull itself up. At high speeds the air foil function of the wing provides most of the lift needed to stay in flight.

WHO ARE WE?

The large amounts of energy required for flight have also led to the evolution of a unidirectional pulmonary system to provide the large quantities of oxygen required for high respiratory rates. This high metabolic rate produces large quantities of radicals in the cells that can damage DNA and lead to tumours. Birds, however, do not suffer from an otherwise expected shortened lifespan as their cells have evolved a more efficient antioxidant system than those found in other animals.

The mechanics of bird flight are similar to those of aircraft, in which the aerodynamic forces sustaining flight are lift and drag, the same principles as for swimming but in a different element. This is produced by the action of air flow on the wing – airfoil shaped so the air provides a net upward force on the wing – while the movement of air is directed downward. In some species additional lift comes from airflow around the bird's body, especially during intermittent flight while the wings are folded or semi–folded.

Aerodynamic drag is the force opposite to the direction of motion, and hence the source of energy loss in flight – *lift-induced drag* (the cost of the wing-producing lift, primarily in the wingtip vortices), and parasitic drag, including skin friction drag from the friction of air and body surfaces and the bird's frontal area. The streamlining of a bird's body and wings reduces these forces.

The *shape* of the wing is important in determining a bird's flight capabilities. Different shapes correspond to different trade-offs between advantages such as speed, low energy use, and manoeuvrability. Two important parameters are the aspect ratio and wing loading. *Aspect ratio i*s the ratio of width to height: high aspect ratio results in long narrow wings that are useful for endurance flight because they generate more lift. *Wing loading* is the ratio of weight to wing area.

Detailed wing morphology can differ even *within* a species. For example, adult turtle doves have longer but more rounded wings than juveniles. This suggests that juvenile wing morphology facilitates their first migrations, while selection for flight manoeuvrability is more important after the juveniles' first moult. Female birds exposed to predators during ovulation produce chicks that grow their wings faster than chicks produced by predator-free females. Their wings are also longer. Both adaptations may make them better at avoiding avian predators.

Birds use three types of flight, distinguished by wing motion.

In *gliding flight*, the upward aerodynamic force is equal to the weight. No propulsion is used; the energy to counteract the energy loss due to aerodynamic drag is either taken from the potential energy of the bird, resulting in a descending flight, or is replaced by rising air

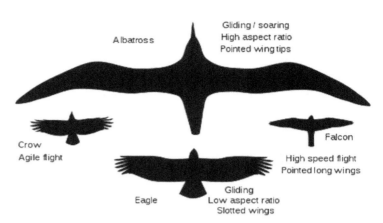

A budgerigar's wings, as on this pet female, allow it excellent manoeuvrability

Wandering albatross in soaring flight

currents ("thermals"): soaring flight. For specialist soaring birds (obligate soarers), flight is strongly related to atmospheric conditions that allow individuals to maximise flight-efficiency and minimise energy costs.

In *flapping* as opposed to gliding, the wings continue to develop lift as before, but the lift is rotated forward to provide thrust, which counteracts drag and increases its speed, which has the effect of also increasing lift to counteract its weight, allowing it to maintain height or to climb.

Flapping involves two stages: the down-stroke, which provides the majority of the thrust, and the up-stroke, which can also (depending on the bird's wings) provide some thrust. At each up-stroke the wing is slightly folded inwards to reduce the energy cost of flapping-wing flight. Birds change the angle of attack continuously within a flap, as well as with speed.

Small birds often fly long distances using *bounding* flight, a technique in which short bursts of flapping are alternated with intervals in which the wings are folded against the body. When a bird's wings are folded, its trajectory is primarily ballistic, with a small amount of body lift. This flight pattern decreases the energy needed by reducing the aerodynamic drag during the ballistic part of the trajectory and increases the efficiency of muscle use.

Several bird species use hovering. True hovering occurs by generating lift through flapping alone, rather than by passage through the air, requiring considerable energy expenditure. This usually confines the ability to smaller birds, but some larger birds, such as kites and ospreys can hover for a short time. Although not a true hoverer, some birds remain in a fixed position relative to the ground or water by flying into a headwind. Most birds that hover have high aspect ratio wings suited to low speed flying.

Hummingbirds are the most accomplished hoverers of all birds, and unique, for unlike in other bird flights their wings are extended throughout the whole stroke, which is a symmetrical figure of eight, with the wing producing lift on both the up-and-down-stroke. Hummingbirds beat their wings at some 43 times per second, with some as many as 80 times per second.

A ruby-throated hummingbird beats its wings many times a second

Taking-off is one of the most energetically demanding aspects of flight, as the bird must generate enough airflow across the wing to create lift.

Small birds do this with a simple upward jump. However, this technique does not work for larger birds, such as albatrosses and swans, which instead must take a running start to generate sufficient airflow. Large birds take off by facing into the wind, or, if they can, by perching on a branch or cliff so they can just drop off into the air.

Landing is a problem for large birds with high wing loads. This problem is dealt with in some species by aiming for a point below the intended landing area (such as a nest on a cliff) then pulling up beforehand. If timed correctly, the airspeed once the target is reached is virtually nil.

A male bufflehead runs on top of the water while taking off

Landing on water is simpler, and the larger waterfowl species prefer to do so whenever possible, landing into wind and using their feet as skids. To lose height rapidly prior to landing, some large birds such as geese indulge in a rapid alternating series of sideslips or even briefly turn upside down.

A wide variety of birds fly together in a symmetric V-shaped or a J-shaped coordinated formation, also referred to as an "echelon", especially during long-distance flight or migration. They probably use this pattern of formation flying to save energy and improve the aerodynamic efficiency. The wingtips of the leading bird in an echelon create a pair of opposite rotating line vortices.

Lesser flamingos flying in formation

The vortices trailing a bird have an underwash part behind the bird, and at the same time they have an upwash on the outside, that hypothetically could aid the flight of a trailing bird. One study suggested that each bird in a V formation of 25 members can achieve a reduction of induced drag and as a result increase their range by 71%. It has also been suggested that birds' wings produce induced thrust at their tips, allowing for proverse yaw and net upwash at the last quarter of the wing. This would allow birds to overlap their wings and gain Newtonian lift from the bird in front. The leader's role is exacting in energy, and on long flights another from time to time takes over.

Waldrapp Ibis

Studies of waldrapp ibises show that they spatially coordinate the phase of wing flapping and show wingtip path coherence when flying in V positions, enabling them to maximally utilise the available energy of upwash over the entire flap cycle. In contrast, birds flying in a stream immediately behind another do not have wingtip coherence in their flight pattern and their flapping is out of phase, as compared to birds flying in patterns.

All in all, bird flying, however it first began, is pretty amazing and has provided many suggestive models for the mechanics of artificial flight.

Albin Kasper Longren was an American aviation pioneer from the state of Kansas. Beginning in 1911, Longren successfully flew airplanes of his own design and construction. Fully self-taught as an aircraft designer and pilot, he built a thriving career as a barnstormer with his own craft, becoming known throughout the Midwest as the "Birdman".

Tools and building

In the evolutionary accounts of *homo sapiens* the use of tools – object or material outside the body, and used for a purpose – has commonly been seen as a turning point that made him ("him") a true human.

This can just refer to exploiting some object in situ – battering something against a stationery stone for instance, or, more deliberately, selecting, picking up and applying some portable object like a pebble or a thorn to a specific purpose. A more progressively human step was seen as not just *using* but *making* a tool, like sharpening and shaping a stick or chipping a stone to make it a handier implement. There are innumerable descriptions in the classic archaeological and historical record to provide evidence of this, leading finally to industrial processes and the manipulation of sophisticated technology.

Birds have nothing remotely like the latter. Indeed, even at a simpler level using tools does not at first sight look like a typical avian characteristic at all. That said however there *are* cases worth attention, many of them only recently identified. Birds utilise parts of their own bodies, especially beaks and claws, to achieve some purpose outside themselves, and make good use of exterior objects too. Who has not seen a thrush crack a snail shell on a stone to get at the meat inside, or birds gathering material of many kinds to build their nests?

Bird tools

So what do we now know about this? Many birds use tools to trap or break open prey. They also make ingenious use of fixed or manipulated devices like thorns to impale their prey. Woodpecker finches, for example, push twigs into trees to catch or impale larvae, while parrots wedge nuts so they can crack the outer shells open without losing the inner contents. Shrikes impale their prey, while other birds use spines or forked sticks to anchor a carcass so they can flay it with their bills.

A woodpecker finch uses a stick to impale a grub, then in the second image has successfully captured it

Many species use prey-*dropping* to get at the food. Gulls for example drop mussels from a height onto a hard surface to break the shell open. Some birds, like Japanese carrion crows, ingeniously take advantage of human activity by dropping nuts in front of cars for them to crack the shells, then swoop down to collect the nuts when the cars have to stop at a red light. The same in America, where crows drop walnuts onto busy streets for the cars to break open – clearly an intelligent innovation by the birds given the relatively recent development of busy traffic covered streets.

Carrion crows too love mussels and are adept at getting the shells open by dropping them from several yards up onto a hard surface. The technique is adapted to fit the nature of the surface, the prey, and the likelihood of theft by others. Thus, north-western crows fly vertically up, release a whelk and at once dive after it, while with American crows, the number of drops to crack a walnut decreased as the height increased, and crows had more success when dropping walnuts onto asphalt than onto soil.

Young gulls, still learning their craft, make their drops from lower heights than their experienced elders and need more tries to be successful. They learn their prey-dropping skills by studying other gulls around them, and are able to refine this behaviour to benefit themselves. They commonly break their prey – black mussels – on hard surfaces like rocks, asphalt, and even roofs of houses and cars, choosing the drop-site both from its effectiveness in breaking open the prey and on the number of competitors other gulls around can trying to steal the dropped prey. Once the drop is made, the gull flies down as quickly as possible to recover it to prevent theft, a common occurrence in prey-dropping. On average, a kelp gull reaches the ground about 0.5 seconds after the prey has landed.

In an interesting case in Central Europe, a two-year-old black-headed gull was seen taking a small swan mussel about 60 feet up into the air to drop on an asphalt road (we don't know how successful this would have been – a crow intercepted it!). The interesting thing is that this technique had not been recorded previously for this species of gulls and was likely due to the presence of large group of prey-dropping hood crows – a case of innovation inspired by observing and copying another species.

Another interesting case was captured in a recent video (https://tinyurl.com/97jmxbb8) of an Egyptian vulture using a pebble as a hammer to break open an ostrich egg. Ostriches lay their eggs in a single nest, the dominant female first, laying around 15 to 20, her subordinates following with 3 to 4 of their own. However, since the top pair of ostriches can only incubate around a dozen eggs effectively, they roll the rest away from the nest – a ring of favourite and nutritious food for any bird skilful enough to break into the eggs. The Egyptian vulture has a special technique for doing so. It picks up round stones in its beak and uses them to hammer the egg shells until they crack. Even ostrich eggs eventually give way. As it turned out, ravens can be even cleverer. Two ravens watched from behind a bush, then flew in at the crucial moment and drove the vultures away – one might say the ravens used the vultures as tools for their own ends.

In a narrow definition of tool use (as the manipulation of physical objects beyond the animal's own body) a bird dropping a shell on a rock would not really be using a *tool*. However, selecting and using a pebble to crack an ostrich egg *would* qualify the Egyptian vulture as a tool user.

Some birds in fact *do* take the additional step of not only using already available objects but also *creating* tools to suit their purposes. Here the striking examples are corvids such as crows, ravens and rooks, as well as parrots and a range of passerines (perching birds). New Caledonian crows for example construct probes out of twigs, wood and sometimes metal wire, to catch or impale larvae or extract insects from logs. New Caledonian crows don't just use single objects as tools; they also construct compound tools by assembling otherwise non-functional elements, while others make their own tools out of, for example, the leaves of pandanus trees. In captivity, a young Española cactus finch learned to imitate this by watching a woodpecker finch in an adjacent cage.

An example of both using and making tools is that of Galapagos finches. If a bird finds inaccessible prey, it flies off to fetch a cactus spine which it then uses in one of three ways: as a goad to drive out an active insect without necessarily touching it; as a spear to impale a slow–moving larva or similar animal; or as an implement with which to push, bring towards, nudge, or otherwise manoeuvre an inactive insect from a crevice. Tools that do not exactly fit the purpose are worked on and adapted, making the bird a "tool maker" as well as a "tool user". Some birds have been observed using tools with novel functional features such as barbed twigs from blackberry bushes, modifying the twig by removing side twigs and leaves in such a way that the barbs could be used to drag the prey out of tree crevices. There have also been reported cases of woodpecker finches choosing and brandishing a twig as a weapon while nuthatches methodically insert pieces of bark pieces underneath an attached bark scale, using it like a lever to expose hiding insects. They sometimes reuse the same piece of bark several times and sometimes even fly short distances carrying the bark flake in their beak. In another example of tool preparation, a captive Tanimbar corella was observed breaking off and shaping splinters of wood and small sticks to create rakes to retrieve an otherwise inaccessible food item on the other side of the aviary mesh.

New Caledonian crows are perhaps the most studied corvid with respect to tool–use. In the wild, they have been observed using sticks as tools to extract insects from tree bark. They poke the insects or larvae until they bite the stick in defence and can then be drawn out, and also manufacture tools from twigs, grass stems or similar plant structures. Captive individuals have been observed to use a variety of materials, including feathers and garden wire. Construction of more complex hooked tools typically involves choosing a forked twig from which parts are removed and the remaining end sculpted and sharpened. New Caledonian crows also use pandanus tools, made from barbed leaf edges of screw pines by precise ripping and cutting.

Hawaiian crow captives use tools to extract food from holes drilled in logs. The juveniles engage in tool use without training or social learning from adults. Other corvid species, such as rooks, also make and use tools in the laboratory with a degree of sophistication, and captive blue jays have been observed using strips of newspaper as tools to obtain food. In other observed cases corvids found stones to put in a vessel of water to raise the surface level to drink from it or access a floating treat, re-enacting Aesop's "Fable of The Crow and the Pitcher".

While young birds in the wild normally learn from their elders how to make stick tools, a laboratory New Caledonian crow ("Betty") was filmed spontaneously improvising a hooked tool from a wire; she had no prior experience of this as she had been hand-reared. New Caledonian crows have also been observed to use an available small tool to get a less easily available longer tool, and then use this to get an otherwise inaccessible longer tool again to get food out of reach of the shorter tools. One bird ("Sam") spent 110 seconds inspecting the apparatus before completing each of the steps without any mistakes – an example of *sequential tool use*, which represents a higher cognitive function compared to many other forms of tool use. Indeed, it has been claimed that tool-making skills like these are more similar to human tool manufacture than those of any other animal.

In Australia, black kites, whistling kites and brown falcons are not only attracted to wildfires, a context where they can source food, but remarkably, use their beaks or talons to carry burning sticks so as to spread the fire. They thus cleverly help themselves, and complicate human efforts to contain fires by creating firebreaks.

Some birds put out bait, a practice possibly learned from humans (unless of course it was the other way round, we don't know). Herons use bread crusts, insects, leaves, and other small objects to attract fish into snatching distance, which they then capture and eat. So do hooded crows. Burrowing owls collect mammalian dung, which they use as a bait to attract dung beetles, a major item of prey. Individuals who have observed fish being fed bread by humans copy this by themselves placing bread in the water to attract fish.

Another example of the way in which birds innovatively exploit relatively recent human activity is the way peregrine falcons cleverly use the gust from trains to help them catch birds flushed out of trees as carriages pass by.

Some birds utilise humans in a different way to help them get *at* their favourite food – and in turn help humans. In Mozambique, Yao people love honey but the wild beehives, high in the treetops, are not easy to locate. Using a trick that has been passed down through generations, they summon the birds by a distinctive *brrr-hm* cry. Once present, the honey guide bird lives up to its name, flitting from treetop to treetop where the beehives are. The birds love to feast on the beeswax within, but cannot crack open the hives to get at it. However, when the humans have harvested the honey they leave the beeswax behind, so the partnership provides both parties with a scrumptious feed – a two-way collaboration between our own species and a bird, from which both partners benefit.

Overall, the genetic predisposition for tool use is refined by individual trial and error and by learning during a sensitive phase early in development, and then builds on thus by observation (including at times learning from a different species), taking account of the specific environment and conditions. For example, the importance of tool use by woodpecker finches differs between vegetation zones. In the arid zone, where food is limited and hard to access, tools are essential for the finches to extract the large, nutritious, insect larvae from tree holes, making tool use more profitable than other foraging techniques. In contrast, in the humid zone, woodpecker finches rarely use tools, since food availability is high and prey easily obtainable. Here, the time and energy costs of tool use would be too high. Sensible!

These are only a few of thousands of recorded cases of bird tool use, often innovative. Scientists have further noted that species that learned new techniques were less vulnerable to extinction than those which did not. Rather than blindly following stereotypical preset behavioural, birds' uses of tools can be, and often are, modified and adapted through learning and experience.

A final point: bird tool uses are directed to *what they want or need* in the context of their lives. Human creatures have, or have developed, additional desires and needs that are presumably worth satisfying and as a result created the tools to achieve these. But, what would be the point of birds doing so when they do not share those needs? Why should they go further than they already do?

In any case it is, all in all, a remarkable repertoire – and one that is, apparently, increasing with both individual and inter-species learning and innovation, going well beyond the common picture of birds as having little or no interest or ability in using tools.

Planning, remembering and learning

The complexity of birds' lives and the settings in which they live mean they have to consider the best way to achieve their purposes – *plan* how to stay safe and fed, and also, as social beings, defend each others' well being.

Protecting their nests and nestlings is one central concern. So, besides the obvious precautions of choosing safe sites and warning off threateners, some birds have developed strategies to mislead potential predators. Skylarks fool watchers by not going straight to their nests when they alight but running several yards always from where it is concealed in the grass. They also have an effective subterfuge to draw off predators by limping along pretending to be wounded and vulnerable so diverting attention away from where their nestlings are hidden. The killdeer bird, found across North America, is the avian equivalent of a scam artist, feigning to be injured or crippled in order to lure a predator toward them and away from their nest of offspring. When the predator gets close enough, the killdeer miraculously "recovers" and disappears.

Birds employ the most astonishing strategies to conceal their young from predators. A female hornbill will seal herself into the nest and stay inside the tree cavity throughout incubation, leaving only a tiny aperture. But she has first been careful to spend a few days testing the male's ability to provide her with food before she committing herself to laying.

Food and its future availability is a continuing preoccupation and a focus for serious planning. Fruit-eating birds in tropical forests depend on trees which fruit at different times of the year. Many species, such as pigeons and hornbills, decide on foraging areas according to the time of the year, hide food from there, then later, when they return, go to the exact locations of their food caches. Honey-loving birds such as hummingbirds optimise their foraging by keeping track of where to find the good and bad flowers. Some birds that gather and hide their food, like various species of jays, hide it up to 2 miles from home, and not only remember where every piece is for up to a year, but also what's in each place and when the food (often bugs or worms) is no longer good to eat. They usually gather far more food than they can eat, and at the end of the year start over again.

Birds that eat the food right away (most of them) apparently don't have, or need, the specialised memory ability of the caching birds.

But they *do* remember encounter they have had with other bird species or mammals, and file the memory away for later use. The sparrows on my friends' porch, for example, have learned to ignore their old, slow cat but are wary of the neighbour's younger, faster cat.

The unassuming Clark's nutcracker has one of the most remarkable memories in the animal kingdom

In the mountains of western North America, each fall nutcrackers use their powerful bills to hammer open ripening pinecones and gather fat and protein-rich seeds in a specialised storage pouch under their tongues. A single bird can carry as many as 90 seeds of their favoured pinyon, limber and whitebark pine. Then one flies off with its load to a south-facing slope, often miles away from the collection site, where winter snow will melt early. There, it buries small groups of seeds in the ground at an average depth of about an inch, and covers them with dirt or gravel. Working almost all day every day from August until December, a single nutcracker can collect as many as 33,000 pine seeds and bury them in more than 2,500 separate hiding places. Using so many storage sites amounts to insurance for the nutcrackers, as some caches are inevitably pilfered by hungry rodents or lost to decay. The caches are, to the human eye, unmarked.

Even more remarkable than the prodigious energy nutcrackers invest in storing food is their *success in finding it again*. They nest in early spring when snow covers the ground and food is scarce and both adult birds and nestlings rely almost entirely on seeds from the remembered stores. Nutcrackers and their young may still be eating the seeds a year after burying them.

Tests have established what caching birds *don't do*. They don't use markings on the ground. They don't smell buried seeds. They don't remember the order in which they created caches. They don't duplicate their flight path when caching and recovering.

What, then, do they do? Recent work by University of Nebraska biologist Alan Kamil and colleagues has shown that the birds note landmarks and are able to understand geometric relationships between them. For example, nutcrackers are able to find seeds buried halfway between two markers even after the markers are moved. They seemingly use abstract relationships, like an equal distance between two landmarks, suggesting that they are very flexible.

Nutcrackers seem to recall some locations better than others, and they excavate the best–remembered sites first. That makes ecological sense: the birds bury more seeds than they need, and only if food supplies remain scarce for a long time will they need to find caches that aren't precisely remembered. This over-storage is significant, as seeds that aren't recovered can sprout into new pines, thereby benefitting both the trees and future generations of nutcrackers.

So, it is clear that in some sense these birds *plan* for the future, concealing food where they know they can find it again when they need it. At the same time memory is linked to need. Nutcrackers and pinyon jays, which both feed almost entirely on stored food while nesting, have excellent memories. Mexican jays and western scrub jays also store seeds, but they nest later in the year when insects are abundant and so don't need to rely so much on their caches. They forget storage locations much more readily than the first two species.

Learning also plays an important role in behaviour. Blue jays for instance rapidly learn to avoid foods that make them sick. Many monarch butterflies contain heart poisons, cardiac glycosides, which they obtain as caterpillars from the milkweed plants they feed on. A jay that has never seen one before will eat it and then suffer a bout of vomiting brought on by the glycosides. Subsequently it will not touch a monarch butterfly or even a viceroy butterfly, which looks very similar. Learning comes in too if a bird has discovered a certain kind of palatable prey: it may form a "search image" for that prey and specialise for a time in eating it.

A bird's feeding preferences are influenced by the diet it learned as a nestling but the changing availability of different kinds of food can also be a factor. Many birds will opportunistically switch to a new food source that suddenly becomes abundant. When seventeen-year cicada ("locust") broods emerge, for example, many birds change from whatever they have been eating to gorge on cicadas. Similarly, Eurasian falcons catch and eat more swifts in cool cloudy weather than in warm sunny weather – the lack of insects in the gloom weakens the swifts, making them easier prey.

Apart from food needs, some birds' visual memory is phenomenal. The common pigeon in particular has an astonishing long-term memory – a single bird can memorise 1,200 pictures. Further, despite the physical differences between birds and other animals (including ourselves), there are similarities in the way their memories work.

Crows, rooks, jays and ravens – hyper-intelligent birds – not only remember human faces of people they have interacted with, but spread thus to other members of their flocks. In one example crows at the University of Washington were caught and banded by researchers wearing rubber masks; at the end of the year eighty of the crows sounded the alarm whenever a human went outside wearing one of the rubber masks. In the case of the African honey guides benefiting from their cooperation with humans in getting access to the honey, the birds remember which people to respond to – only a few have the skills and inclination to crack open the hives for them.

All migrating birds remember how to get to their home nesting site, and they use the same exact site (bush, tree, reed bed) year after year until either the bird or the site are no longer there.

Planning and memory depend on the species of bird and the situation. They remember what they need to and very likely nothing more – why would they?

Nests

And then there is nest building. Here birds really do excel, arguably leading rather than following us humans.

Nest building is the best-known skill of birds and one of their key adaptive advantages. What they do in constructing their homes can indeed be regarded as a form of tool using: skilfully manipulating chosen material to fit their purposes. They use a variety of materials from the natural or man–made world and with great craft work them into complex and sophisticated constructions. The nests they fashion help regulate temperature and reduce predation risks, thus increasing the chance that offspring will live to adulthood.

There is good reason for this skill. Unlike with the human reproductive, a female bird carry eggs with her – flying would, to say the least, be harder and require more energy. Just as an aircraft cannot fly if it is overweight, all female birds must dispense with the weight of a fertile egg as soon as it is formed. And because eggs are such a protein-rich high-nutrition prize to all sorts of predators, birds must find a secure place to hatch and protect them.

Although birds' eggs appear fragile, they are in fact extremely robust. The oval shape applies the same rules of engineering as an arched bridge; the convex surface can withstand considerable pressure without breaking. This is essential if the egg is not to crack under the weight of the sitting bird. It takes 26 pounds of pressure to break a swan's egg and 120 pounds to smash the egg of an ostrich.

Finding somewhere to safely place and hatch the eggs and raise their young to the point of independence, is a challenge birds have solved in many clever ways. They use artistry, intricate design and complex engineering. The diversity of nest architecture has no equal in the animal kingdom.

Many birds build isolated, inconspicuous nests, hidden away inside the vegetation to avoid detection. Some are so successful at hiding their nests that even investigating human observers have hardly ever found them – birds like hummingbirds and manakins, for example. One secretive nester, the marbled murrelet, locates its nest high in the canopy of ancient douglas firs over 300 years old.

One of the most remarkable ploys of putting its nest out of most predators' reach is demonstrated by African palm-swifts. They use their own saliva to glue the nest, a little pad of feathers, to the vertical underside of a palm frond. The two eggs are also glued to the nest and the parents incubate them by turns, clinging to the nest.

Although nests are primarily used for breeding, they are also sometimes reused in the non-breeding season for roosting and some species build dormitory or roost nests used only for roosting. Most birds build a new nest each year, though some refurbish their old nests. The large eyries of some eagles are platform nests have sometimes been used and refurbished for years.

Nests vary from simple depressions in the ground ("scrapes") and unstructured collections of branches to elaborately woven pendants and spheres. A few species do not build nests at all but lay eggs directly onto rock ledges or bare soil without modifying the area – it generally works for them. As against this weaver birds fashion truly elaborate nests with strands of grass tied into knots.

Most bird nests lie somewhere in the middle, with the majority building cup-shaped nests using some combination of mud, twigs and leaves, and feathers, their type, location and architecture influenced not just by the species and its culture but also by local topography and resources.

Some birds build their nests in trees, some (such as vultures, eagles and many seabirds) on rocky ledges, others on the ground or in burrows. Some build on cactuses. Bushtits and bullock orioles suspend their nests from the tips of slender branches. The oropendolas take hanging nests to the extreme, constructing pouches up to nearly two yards tall using hanging vines as their base. This hanging nest is attached to thin tree branches, discouraging predation.

Other species seek out crevices and use buildings or birdhouses when tree holes are not available.

Rooks and other large birds can afford to nest where they can be seen, but most birds are more

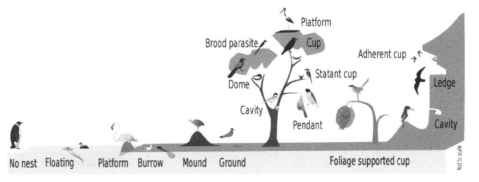

Intricate weaver bird nests

secretive. Blackbirds, robins and song thrushes build nests in the classic design of neat cups of woven grasses and small twigs, camouflaged with moss and lined with mud. The birds are careful about approaching their chosen nest site, and stop to check they are not being watched before they plunge into a hedge or shrub.

Typical bird nests range from under an inch in size (hummingbirds) to 2 yards (eagles) in diameter. The largest nest on record was made by a pair of bald eagles. It was 3 yards in diameter, 6 yards deep and estimated to weigh more than 2 tonnes. The lightest bird nests weigh only a few grams. Incubation mounds of the malleefowl can reach heights of 5 yards and widths of 11 yards; the bird uses as much as 300 tonnes of material in their nest construction.

The simplest type of nest is no nest at all. Nightjars do not make even a scrape. They lay two eggs directly onto the ground while short-eared owls just lay them on some trampled vegetation.

Next up is a simple scrape. Many waders, such as plovers, lay in a scrape on bare ground, relying on the cryptic colouration of their eggs to protect them from predation. The potoos lay a single egg on top of a broken off tree still tump, typically where an upward-pointing branch has died and fallen off, leaving a small scar or knot-hole. The bird sits on top of the stump with its head pointing to the sky. In this position it looks – good camouflage – like just a part of the dead tree.

Even riskier are the "nests" of fairy terns, who lay one egg on a branch or a rock face, generally an area too small to support 2 eggs. Laying the egg in a position where it won't roll off is tricky and young birds often lose their first attempts before they get the hang of choosing a safe spot.

*Fairy tern nurturing its young
– with no nest*

Fairy terns have two adaptations that help them survive this seemingly precarious nesting habit. The adults have evolved to be very careful when settling on and getting off the egg – both sexes incubate the egg. The second adaptation is that young fairy terns have disproportionally large feet and very sharp claws which help them hang on.

Other bird species lay their eggs directly on the ground. Some auks, including the common murre, thick-billed murre, razorbill and guillemots lay their eggs on the narrow rocky ledges they use as breeding sites. For many years the theory was that eggs are pointed at one end so that they roll in an arc when disturbed.

However, a study published in *Auk: Ornithological Advances, 2018*, dispelled this widely held belief and shows instead that guillemot eggs are inherently *more stable* on the sloping ledges that guillemots, for example, often breed on.

The simple nest of a great black-backed gull

Some crevice-nesting species, including ashy storm-petrel, pigeon guillemot, Eurasian eagle-owl and Hume's tawny owl, lay their eggs in the relative shelter of a crevice in the rocks or a gap between boulders, but provide no additional nest material so no building techniques are needed. Brood parasites like the New World cowbirds, the honeyguides, and many of the Old World and Australasian cuckoos, lay their eggs in the active nests of other species – again no nest building needed. Others just make themselves at home on a pile of stones,

Female Adelie penguin incubates in her simple nest made of stones

The masters of *no*-nest building have to be emperor penguins. Instead of building nests they tuck their eggs and chicks between their feet and folds of skin on their lower bellies. This is in fact very practical as they are then able to move about while incubating.

They nest inland in the Antarctic during winter, when the temperature can fall to less than –30 degrees C. When the female has laid her single egg, she leaves for the coast to feed. Meanwhile the male takes care of the egg by moving it up onto the top of his feet. He has special folds of skin on his belly which enfold the egg, keeping it safe against all the severity of the elements. Here he stays – a portable nest with an egg on his feet – for the next 60 days, without a meal until his mate returns and the egg hatches. During this time he has maintained the internal temperature of the egg at 40 degrees C, as much as 80 degrees C higher than the surrounding ambient temperature.

Emperor penguins breed during the harshest months of the Antarctic winter, and their mobility allows them to form huge huddles which help them withstand the extremely high winds and low temperatures of the season. Without the ability to share body heat (temperatures in the centre of tight groups can be as much as 10C above the ambient air temperature), the penguins would expend far more energy trying to stay warm, and breeding attempts would probably fail.

A common example of a simple platform nest are those constructed by many doves and pigeons. The ruddy quail dove's nest is made from a simple lattice with just enough twigs to support the egg which can often be seen through the nest from beneath. Sometimes the bird adds a flimsy lining of grass and rootlets, in other cases a more complete lining.

A well-known example of building a more substantial platform nest is that of the European white stork which has for centuries nested on chimneys and specially erected platforms across Europe. More complicated than the previous nests, it consists of sticks interwoven then plastered with mud. A depression in the middle is often lined with grass or paper.

Mute swans' nests are an example of a different form of simple nest construction.

Once the site is chosen and the vegetation flattened, the eggs are laid and the female swan builds the nest by simply dragging material within reach to make a rampart around her.

The most spectacular simple nests are those built by eagles, some so heavy that they damage the tree supporting them.

The largest nests on record are those of golden eagles who often build on top of the previous year's nest. This results in huge structures often containing more than a ton of material. Fortunately, golden eagles prefer rocky alpine crags as nest sites which can support these massive structures more easily than a tree.

The next step up from a simple platform nest is a cup-shaped nest – the commonest type.

And one that most people consider the typical "birds nest". They have a definite inside as well as an outside and the inside is normally lined. They need more effort to construct, but convey more protection to the eggs and young birds.

Song thrush cup-shaped nest

The smallest cup-shaped nests are those of the woodstar hummingbirds who build perfectly shaped thimble sized nests of moss and cobwebs. Often the female bird flies during the whole construction, hovering while building up the shape. Cup-shaped nests are usually built of a mixture of substances. Redwings build nests of leaves, grasses and fine twigs cemented together and then lined with moss and feathers.

Not all cup nests have a soft lining. Female song thrushes line their nests with mud, dung and rotten wood cemented together to form a hard inner surface.

At the other extreme from the hummingbird delicate nests are the large scraggly structures built by crows. Rooks, one of the most observable nest builders, building their large nests at the top of the bare trees by the roadsides. They start by collecting sticks and dropping them on the branches they have chosen as their home. To begin with, the twigs drop through, but with time, lodge in the branches of the tree and a rather unruly nest begin to form. The initial outside, built of twigs and grass cemented together with mud, is larger than the adult bird. Within this rough exterior, a deep cup lined with moss and feathers is made. The nests often look rough and ready, but inside are warm and comfortable.

Crows build very well and their nests last for several years. Unlike the closely related but larger raven they never reuse a nest but other birds like kestrels are happy to use them once the crow has finished with them.

Enclosed bird nests are basically an extended cup nest, where the basic cup has deeper walls and a roof with an entrance hole.

Domed or enclosed nests offer more protection for the eggs and young than a simple cup, better shielded from the elements and from predators.

The simplest domed nests like those of chiffchaffs or magpies have only a loose roof, while wrens and dippers build more solid domes. Many domed bird nests are very intricate and solidly constructed however.

They can be small and beautiful, such as the nests of the long-tailed tits who camouflage the outside with lichens and line the inside with hundreds of thousands of feathers. An unusual example of a domed nest is built by rufous-breasted castle builders who create a dumbbell shape with a tube connecting both chambers, only one of which is used to rear the young.

Hanging birds' nests, particularly woven ones, are perhaps the most amazing of bird architectures. They look very beautiful and require great skill to build. Some are basically cup-nests slung from an overhead bough by a few cobweb supports, such as those built by goldcrests and firecrests. An interesting variation is the hummingbird's hanging best with only

A nesting colony of the sociable weaver bird may house hundreds of individuals

a single support cable. To help keep it stable it has a streamer of grass and cobwebs hanging down below the nest.

Tailorbirds, well so named, stitch leaves together to provide cover for their nest sites. They build large communal nesting places within which there are many individual nests, dividing it by constructing walls of grass on a base of large sticks. At the entrances to the nest, they place sharp sticks to ward off intruders. A single communal site can be 2 yards high, and sometimes as many as 300 mating pairs reside in it. Other birds often build their own nests on top of weaver nest sites.

The hammerkopf builds what must be the most extraordinary construction in the bird world. The huge, domed nest is up to six feet high, can weigh up to 50 kg, and is strong enough to support a man's weight. It is preferably built in the fork of a tree, often over water, but if necessary, on a bank, a cliff, a human-built wall or dam, or on the ground. A pair starts by making a platform of sticks held together with mud, then builds walls and a domed roof. A mud-plastered entrance 5-7 ins wide in the bottom leads through a 2 foot tunnel to a nesting chamber big enough for the parents and young. These nests take between 10 and 14 weeks to build, and need around 8000 sticks or bunches of grass to complete. Nesting material may still be added by the pair after the nest has been completed and eggs have been laid. Much of the nesting material added after completion is not sticks, but an odd collection of random items including bones, hide, and human waste.

Tools of the trade

A pouch containing a tailorbird's nest

How do birds, with, apparently, only beaks as tools, turn these basic components into homes secure enough to take a growing family of nestlings vying for their parents' attentions and stretching their wings?

Here is one example. A tailorbird takes a large growing leaf or several small ones and with its sharp bill pierces holes into the opposite edges. It then grasps spider silk, silk from cocoons, or plant fibres with its bill, pulls this "thread" through the two holes, and knots it to prevent it from pulling through, repeating this till the leaf or leaves forms a pouch or cup in which the bird then builds its nest. The leaves are sewn together in such a way that the upper surfaces are outwards making the structure difficult to see. The punctures made on the edge of the leaves are minute so do not cause browning of the leaves, further aiding camouflage.

The processes used by tailorbirds have been classified as sewing, riveting, lacing and matting. Once the stitch is made, the fibres fluff out on the outside and in effect they are more like rivets. Sometimes the fibres from one rivet are extended into an adjoining puncture and appear more like sewing. There are many variations in the nest and some may altogether lack the cradle of leaves. It is believed that only females perform this sewing behaviour.

Given the intricacy and sophistication of the process, it is remarkable that birds only spend a small part of their year – often only a few days – building nests, and yet know to build to the design that is unique to their species.

Beaks are good tools for building, supplemented by larger bodily movements. It's a delicate business, the weaving in of new material to create the nest cup. A blackbird will land on the base of the nest and lay the next strand of grass or twig on the top. She then turns in the nest and carefully weaves this new strand into the side of the cup. It is her turning action that leaves the inside of the nest completely smooth and well compacted, ready to take eggs and chicks. She continues until the cup is complete and then visits ponds or puddles and collects mud to strengthen the inside of the nest.

In the majority of nest-building species the female does most or all of the nest construction. In others both partners contribute; sometimes the male builds the nest and the hen lines it. In polygynous species the male usually does most or all of the nest building while in some species the young from previous broods also act as helpers for the adults. The nest is sometimes part of the courtship display, as with weaver birds: an ability to build and maintain high quality nests may appeal to females.

They select and carry objects for future use and manipulate them by bending and twisting them so as to shape the nest and prevent the eggs from rolling away. Different species go about nest site selection in various ways. With gulls both partners together decide on the site. In some species the pair work together but the female takes a definite lead, for example blackbirds and red-necked phalarope (quite surprising as once the site has been chosen, the female lays her eggs and departs – leaving the male to do the incubation).

In many species the male bird's skill at nest building is a sign of his suitability as a mate; he invests huge effort in the task, then the female will carefully peruse the design and quality of the nest he has built; if she likes it, she will move in; if not, the nest may be discarded or destroyed by the male.

Female red-winged blackbird carrying building material for the nest

Collecting nest material at Lake Naivasha, Kenya

Males of the workaholic house wren (North and South America) – build up to twelve nests to attract females and continue to build new nests until a female chooses just one of them while he uses another to roost in.

In other species such as dunnocks the female chooses the site and builds the nest, while among blue tits, European sparrows and wrens, the male decides on the site and then tries to attract the female to it. And then, just to prove that variety is the spice of life, Scottish crossbills have no set patterns at all: sometimes the male leads, sometimes the female.

Birds will use any material that they can carry away to build their nest – leaves, sticks, mosses, lichens, mud, feathers, human hair, even metal or plastic pieces. The Australian yellow-faced honeyeater sometimes filches the thick fur from the back of a koala to line its nest.

Gathering and building techniques vary. One is *"sideways throwing"* – a simple single movement to get nesting material to the nest (this is limited to ground nesters). *"Sideways building"* is similar, but involves more care in the placing of the material and results in a better constructed nest. These two techniques are used by many ducks, geese, gulls, petrels, pheasants, swans, and waders.

Physically carrying material to the nest site is the next step up and is carried out by all the remaining nest building birds. At its simplest, penguins carry a stone in their bills a few yards to the nest site. At its most complex it involves birds searching out particular substances such as cobwebs or feathers to bring to the nest.

Once material is got to the site, it has to be incorporated into the nest. For ground nesting species, this can be as simple as just picking it up. For tree nesting species, it usually involves some degree of interweaving the individual items until they form some sort of matrix. This can be fairly straightforward in the platform nests of pigeons, but reaches great sophistication in weavers' nests where material is *sewn* together and a considerable degree of manipulatory skill needed.

The many species of weaver birds are renowned for their carefully woven hanging nests, hung either from the tip of a branch or leaf, or between two twigs, globular with a single entrance hole. Weaver birds also construct kidney-shaped and retort–shaped nests which are basically globular nests with an entrance tunnel. Whatever their shape, nearly all weavers make their nests out of grass and their nests are truly woven, with the bird moving from side-to-side, poking part of the strand of grass through the wall from the side and then pulling it completely through from the other.

The edible-nest swiftlets of South-East Asia also make a nest entirely from their own saliva. The swiftlets build the nests high up on the roofs of a cave, hard basket–shaped cups made of concentric rings of a protein-rich goo secreted during the breeding season by the male's enlarged salivary glands. He dribbles long sticky strands, using his beak as a shuttle to weave a cup-shaped bracket onto the cave wall (unfortunately for the bird, some people regard the nests as a delicacy). Of the birds that nest on the ground, a few use holes either opening onto a cliff edge or vertical edge of a river bank, or on relatively flat ground. Birds nesting on cliff edge holes include house martins, sand martins and kingfishers, while white-whiskered soft-wings nest in holes dug into flat ground. They line the nests to some extent so they are generally dry, well-protected, homes.

Excavating your own holes is hard work and many birds are happy to take possession of someone else's efforts. Thus, the shelduck and the manx shearwater prefer to nest in abandoned rabbit holes and the sharp-tailed stream creepers in rodent burrows that are often in the edges of open sewers earning the bird the fitting nickname of 'President of Filth' in Brazilian shanty towns!

Mud or earth is not the only place to make a hole and many birds nest in holes found – or excavated in – trees, cacti and even termite nests. Making a nest in a hole that already exists in a tree is not really an architectural feat, as it involves little effort by the bird. Still, holes in trees, alive or dead, make excellent nest sites and numerous birds use them. Some, like the blue tits, redstarts, flycatchers and starlings, use existing holes and make little modification except to add some lining. Others, like the many hole nesting parrots and nuthatches, modify existing holes.

Malachite kingfisher coming out its nesting hole

Fewer birds excavate their own holes in trees but of those that do the woodpeckers, with their impressive hammer-drill impersonations, are by far the best known.

Eurasian nuthatch at nesting cavity

The champion tree hole nesters are hornbills who nest in hollows in trees. This is not as simple as it sounds. The great Indian hornbills for example, nearly a yard from bill-tip to tail-end, likes to nest between twenty and forty-five yards up the tree trunk, so. only nest in trees which have a diameter greater than one or two yards at this height. Since trees this large are now rare in many forests, this puts serious pressure on the breeding capability of these birds.

Both males and females help excavate the hole, which needs to be quite extensive to house the female and several chicks for some weeks. Once it is large enough to accommodate the female, she gets inside and helps the male wall up the entrance with a mixture of guano, woodchips and mud.

The female stays in the hole until the young are ready to fledge. Only a small slit is left in the mud wall, to allow the male to feed the female and her young. During this time she can not only raise the chicks in great security, but also moult all her feathers in one go. Hornbills are long-lived birds and mate for life, so the male has a considerable vested interest in keeping the female well-fed.

Nesting in holes may be secure from many predators and much of the weather, but has one drawback: the warm, humid conditions are ideal conditions for various avian pests and nest parasites such as bird and feather lice, ticks and fleas, and parasite loads in nest holes build up rapidly. Hornbills never use the same hole twice and the need to escape these pests may have something to do with this.

Other favourite sites for nest holes are cacti, many of which grow as large as small trees, and termite nests. Each of these provides an interesting example of commensalism (association between two organisms in which one benefits and the other derives neither benefit nor harm). The orange-fronted parakeet of Central America, to take one example, nests almost exclusively in termite mounds but unlike other creatures nesting there do not seal off the nest hole from the rest of the mound. Soldier termites can thus wander around the birds nest and remove the young birds' faeces and any parasites they can find. Obviously, this is good for the parakeet.

Gila woodpecker breeding pair taking turns at feeding young in saguaro cactus

The second relationship is quite extraordinary. The gila woodpecker nests in holes which it excavates in the famous giant saguaro cactus of North America. In the same hole, nests the elf owl, is tolerated because it has the amazing habit of catching western blind snakes and bringing them alive back to the nest. The snakes are insectivores, so benefit by having a cosy home and free food in the form of avian parasites. The woodpecker benefits because it gets a reduced parasite loading, thus improving the health of its young. The owl gets not only a reduced parasite loading and a free nest site, but also protection for its young while it is off hunting at night when the woodpecker is roosting in the hole. Incredible all round!

Then there are the strange Solomon Islands mound nests where the already-mated female megapodes scrub hens leave the forest where they have lived all year and come down to the beach to look for an area of sand that is heated from below by geothermal energy, as well as from above by the sun.

Into this they dig a hole about two feet deep, and after testing the temperature of the sun with special heat sensors on their tongues (about 33 degrees C is best), they lay their eggs and fill the hole in. The females return to the forest and expend no further effort on their offspring's behalf.

This and similar systems such as the use of hot springs on Celebes and rotting tree stumps on other Solomon Islands, involve no building effort at all. In Australia and Papua New Guinea megapodes use heat generated by composting organic matter to hatch their eggs.

Malleefowl have extremely complex nesting habits. A male starts constructing an incubation mound months before the breeding season. He first scrapes a hole in the ground (megapodes = big feet) about one and a half feet deep. On top of this he piles all the vegetation he can find, as well as nearby topsoil. The resulting nest mound reaches an amazing one yard high and five yards across.

Malleefowl on top of its nest mound

Though a number of birds build their nests at the water's edge, several groups building them actually *in* or *on* the water as floating or aquatic nests.

Coots build nests which though surrounded by water, have a foundation of vegetation which reaches the ground below. Horned coots, who breed on mountain lakes in the Andes where water weed is scarce, build a foundation of stones before the actual nest. Grebes, more adventurously, build their nests in shallow water and though often anchored at one or two points they are basically floating on the water. This is necessary because grebes, primarily water birds, are very clumsy on land and find life works better if they can swim right onto the nest.

Two other groups of birds build nests which are completely afloat. These are the jacanas who build extremely flimsy nests that often sink into the water while the bird is sitting (fortunately eggs are waterproof, so this doesn't harm them). The others are the three species of marsh terns who build nests of broken reeds in water up to four feet deep, sometimes anchored to nearby vegetation.

A jacanas nest floats precariously on the river

And then, there is building with mud. This is a common resource and it makes sense that birds use it.

Flamingos, for one, well known and colourful birds, make their nests from mud and faeces in the middle of the soda lakes of Africa, basically hollow mounds with a depression in the centre. They are not built all at once, but some mud is built up above water level and as this dries more is put on top. They can be as much as eighteen inches high with no lining except the mud.

Many birds build cup-shaped mud nests on trees. They often mix straw or grass with the mud, making them stronger when dried – much like ancient bricks. Normally, these bird's nests are lined with grasses, leaves, moss and feathers.

Oven bird mud nest

In South America, the two species of oven birds build perhaps the most complicated mud nests of all-globular and often on tree stumps, about the size of a football. On one side is a domed entrance which leads to a passage that curves around the left hand side, before going into the central chamber. The inner chamber is well lined and comfortable.

The best known mud nest builders are the swallows and martins who all over the world labour during the spring to build their hemispherical nests on the edges of cliffs and under the eaves of houses. They collect the mud in small pellets moistened with saliva before being applied to the wall or existing nest. As with other mud nesting birds, they then line the nests with dried grass and feathers. Swallows and martins, in Europe at least, build only in the morning, spending the afternoon feeding. This means that each day's work gets a chance to dry out and become strong before new mud is added, otherwise the whole thing would collapse under its own weight.

Edible nest of the Swiftlet made from saliva

Perhaps the strangest of all are the edible nests built by the species of swiftlets who nest in caves and build their nests of saliva. To make them even more amazing, they often nest in pitch dark caves where they use echolocation like bats.

We humans have our industrial processes and products and our sophisticated technologies, birds have their astounding nest-building skills. Who is to say which is the more to be prized?

Social beings

Like humans and some other mammals, birds are very much social beings, not only in parenting and nurturing their families, but in working, playing, migrating, navigating, flocking – in short in *living, being* – together.

From earliest infancy, even in the egg, the young birds are with others. They learn with and from others, they meet and feed with others, they sing-duet with others or work jointly with them. Being social, means they have to take account of others' actions whether in joining a migrating flock, in courtship rituals, nurturing their young, or defending their territory against others.

It starts even before birth. A few species lay single eggs but for the majority of birds their first experience is of being in a nest with other, both before and for several weeks after birth. Being in a social group is their natural and expected experience.

So, the chicks, in the nest with many siblings, wait together for the food the parents bring – competition perhaps but confident that each will have what is needed and that they will grow together close to their siblings – fed and tended and loved by (in most cases) two cooperating parents.

The youngsters leave the nest at about the same time as they fledge from chick fluffiness and develop wing feathers, then – trial and error – learn to glide and fly while the parents keep a watching eye, protecting and feeding them, still a group, on the ground, until they gradually learn to fend for themselves.

Through experiment, watching, play, and mimicry young birds learn the ways of their species' culture which, as with humans, is likely to vary from place to place. They pass much, maybe all, of their time in a group, feeding, playing, observing the world. The parents keep a watching eye on them – fully social beings.

Time passes and the group become ready for the next stage, time for the young bird to seek a mate. Then, specially for males, come lavish courtship displays, choice of mate, pairing and a new cycle of nest building, parenting and nurturing.

Who has not marvelled at some bird's courtship display? Or a peacock's amazing show-off colours or enjoyed the sight of paired birds in flight, or talking together, or, it seems, kissing, or at their nests in love and loyalty as well as companionship.

Birds are largely though not exclusively socially monogamous at least for a season (not necessarily sexually so however). There is also sometimes polygyny, a male mating with many, females or, very occasionally, the other way round (polyandry).

Avian monogamy is well known, famously for, for example, barn owls, black vultures, golden eagles, macaws, geese and penguins.

The lovingly entwined necks of a swan pair in the shape of heart have become classic images of faithful love. Indeed, if one perishes the other has been documented as dying of heartbreak or at least grieving for many seasons before – perhaps – accepting a new mate. Many people were moved, and even a children's book created, by the story (https://tinyurl.com/4pmt9sz9) of a London mute swan who mourned the death of her mate for four years when he was killed after hitting a building while they were flying together in 2016. The heartbroken bird spent the next four years grieving, searching for him all through nearby nesting grounds and laying unfertilised eggs as she pined for her lost love, refusing all offers from other eager would-be mates.

Finally, she was rescued and placed in a swan sanctuary where she was put in the same pen as a male called Wallace. Wallace took her under his wing – and at last she had found a new love. By now the loving pair, back in her home Highgate pond, are proudly caring for a nest of cygnets. Love between pairs has its costs, for there is death and suffering too, the price of' social caring.

A swallow finds his mate dying in the road, brings her food to try to revive and comfort her, watches over her, protecting – and finally has to accept it (it is surely not only human beings whose hearts break).

To move on through the life cycle, it is now time for bringing up the next generation. *Two*-parent care is the norm in birds, occurring in more than 90% of avian species, whereas in other animal groups if biparental care occurs at all it is much less common than single parent care. In fact, in only a few mammal species (less than 5%) do males provide any direct care of their young while in the vast majority of bird species males share the

parenting duties. True, females shoulder the full parenting load in a few avian families, such as hummingbirds but in almost all other bird species, the males stay around to help. They share the duties of nest-building, incubate eggs, feed brooding females and the chicks, train their young for independent life. Birds, in short, birds have a system of parenting not unlike our own, despite being separated from us by some 300 million years of evolutionary history.

One variation is that found among goldcrests, Their females often lay a second clutch of eggs before the first chicks have developed flight feathers so as to be able leave the nest. The male continues to care for the first brood whilst the female begins building a new nest.

Birds take on rearing their children with variety and flair – and, it would seem with love. Most young birds are brought up in two-parent nests; others just by the mother, some just by dad; some are raised by foster parents, still others shared in large group settings. The parents may be mated for life or just the season, but they are committed until the young are ready to be on their own.

A few birds – chickens and their relations – do things differently: barnyard fowl, grouse, turkeys, pheasants and quail (all descendants, it is said, from *Tyrannosaurus rex*). These males mate by occupying a territory and copulating with as many females they can. The father's responsibility then ends and the mother is on her own to raise the brood – she is, indeed, ("as a hen gathers her chicks …") famous for her devotion.

But leaving fowls aside, how do birds take care of their eggs and their young? Before anything else they have, with amazing skill, built a nest to protect the eggs from bad weather and predators. At least one parent, most often both, is there to care of the young ones until they are ready to fly, and often to an extent after.

In most species, parents invest profoundly in their offspring as a mutual effort, the majority of them socially monogamous for the duration of the breeding season.

Penguins are a striking example of complex alternating two-parent care. Parents take turns feeding the chicks, going back to the sea to feed themselves, ready to pass it in to the chicks. The first eggs hatch in August, and the fathers provide a curdlike food from their esophagi to support the chicks for about two weeks. Then the females return to care for the babes.

The males, who have withstood ice and cold throughout the harsh Antarctic winter, are relieved from their egg-sitting duties to head to the sea to feed. The females regurgitate food for their babies until they can no longer produce it, then they head back to the sea to refuel, leaving the chicks alone to wait for the males to return. Soon they reappear, nourished and able to feed the chicks. Interestingly, penguins recognise and feed only their own chicks, and the males find their babies by listening for distinctive calls.

All in all two-parent care is by far the most common avian form. The mating pair contribute equally to feeding and guarding the offspring, and hatchlings benefit. Each parent tries to find a mate who will not desert the nest and has high qualities that showcase their parental skills.

Wire-tailed swallow feeding offspring

In bi-parental care, the male generally provides the food while the female is a caretaker. Both ensure the survival of the offspring. The female cares for her young by covering them to keep them warm, shielding them from the sun and rain, and guarding them from predation. The male may also feed the female, who in turn regurgitates the food to the chicks. Non-breeding adults or juveniles (as with acorn woodpeckers) sometimes also contribute to the care, collaborating with the parents.

Polyandry in Northern Jacana

In polyandry, one female mates with multiple males (one male mates with only one female), a system which occurs in under 1% of all bird species. Parental roles are reversed and males provide most of the care. In simultaneous polyandry, the female dominates a territory of several small nests with two or more males, who take care of the offspring. Parental roles are unique, since in contrast to other species, the females compete for the males, who then take on most of the parental care.

Northern jacanas are one example. A female, mates with the males in her territory, often on the same day. In return, the female helps to defend the territory. No copulation occurs during the incubation period and during the first six weeks after the offspring are hatched. If the eggs are lost, the female mates with the male once again.

In sequential polyandry (the commoner form) as among certain types of red and red–necked phalaropes and spotted sandpipers in South America, a female mates with a male and lays her eggs. She then departs, leaving the male to care for the clutch while she repeats the process with another male.

WHO ARE WE?

There is a clear distinction between the roles of the parents among Iberian rock sparrows. The female incubates the eggs for 11-14 days before they hatch, then feeds the offspring while the male teaches them to fly and leave the nest, usually within 18 days of birth. Rock sparrows mostly bring one food item per trip, other times guarding the nest.

Providing food is a more onerous task than it may seem as even for their own food the parents may need hundreds of caterpillars to keep them going, let alone the extra needed for the very young. One pair of tiny birds like blue tits for instance have to find up to 1,000 caterpillars every single day – that's a lot of flying back and forth, and the amount of energy used up in the search for food is incredible. A single pair of breeding chickadees have to find 6,000 to 9,000 caterpillars to rear just one clutch of young.

And cuckoos who lay an egg in another bird's nest and leave them to bring up the young? Birds only behave brutally or with deceit – like these cuckoo parasites – because it works in terms of their own survival and life style. Against this there are countless examples of devoted pairing and parenting.

Among white-winged choughs for example four adults are deployed to feed one young, because the beetle grubs they eat are so difficult to find. But they will also kidnap young from another family, enticing them away by spreading their wings like a toreador's cloak. The youngster is fed for the first season, then recruited into the feeding team in the next year. The result is a bigger "family", capable of raising more young.

In British Colombia the Barrows goldeneye also choose the extended family option. The female goldeneye will chase another female off the lake, but is happy to let the rival's abandoned offspring join her family. She may end up with 20 ducklings in tow, only half of them her own. This is not as altruistic as it seems. By then she does not have to feed them and if a pike attacks, the odds are 2 to 1 against hers' being eaten.

In Australia, the magpie geese family is often headed by a male and two egg-laying females. When the time comes to conduct their young across a river to the lagoon where they feed, the three parents will snap at marauding crocs, a act of heroism that could easily lose them their heads.

And then there is the care shown by rosella parrot parents. Their eggs hatch over about five days, so at first there is a noticeable size difference between their chicks. You might expect the older ones to win. But, unlike some other birds, these parrots are scrupulously fair in feeding and make sure every nestling receives its proper ration. Sometimes the eldest will even share its food with the youngest and weakest. The result is a truly balanced family: after three weeks of this systematic care, things will have evened out and the nestlings will all be the same size.

Perhaps the biggest and happiest of bird families are the Arabian babblers of Israel. These birds display an admirable family togetherness. They all play a part in feeding the baby birds.

Birds' parenting is truly impressive, but in fact birds are not a lot more virtuous or dutiful in their home–making then humans. It had often been thought that birds were the animal kingdom's best representatives of the romantic virtues.

The courtship of birds, and their apparent togetherness, has long inspired poets, songsmiths and advertising copywriters. We assumed birds don't cheat – but ... they sometimes do! Although around 90 per cent of bird species form a parental pair, at least for a given breeding season – a higher figure than among other creatures – there is more deception than was ever suspected. Monogamy is not an instinct hard-wired into birds' brains, as was thought. Even those considered as paragons of fidelity will indulge in a fling if the situation permits. DNA fingerprinting has revealed that as many as a fifth of the eggs produced by female birds believed to be monogamous had not, after all, been sired by their regular partners, devoted fathers though they then become. Scientists now know that females can two-time, even practice divorce. There can be jealousy, there are "home-wreckers".

Set against this are the undoubted cases of undying selfless devotion to a chosen mate and, whatever the background, whoever the biological father, the continuing time–consuming parenting.

Next comes the stage of teaching the young to fly. Fledglings usually begin trying to fly when at about two weeks old, and even after have started to leave the nest, they are not on their own. The parents are nearby, keeping a watchful eye on their offspring and still providing food.

Some birds leave their nests before they can fly, while others, mainly cavity nesters like woodpeckers, stay put until they master the necessary skill. Leaving before they can fly is a means of survival. A nest full of young birds is an easy target for predators, so having the fledglings spread out gives them a greater chance of surviving.

So now is the moment when the fledglings leave the nest. This is not as straightforward as it may sound as birds don't know how to fly when they hatch. Learning to fly is a gradual process, and often involves some trial and error for the young birds because flying needs not just instinct but also learning and practice.

If the fledglings are too long trying their wings, the parents may push them out. And then, just as a baby's first steps are interrupted by frequent stumbles and falls but they don't really hurt themselves, the young birds try it out. They don't learn to fly in a day, Often, it starts by falling out of the nest and making the long trip back to it. Eventually, the young birds come to realise that falling from the nest is easier if they spread their wings. Once they learn to *spread* their wings, flapping them is the next step, and soon that flapping becomes flight.

But even then, it isn't with the ease we are accustomed to seeing birds fly with. They still need practice. They have to learn how to take off and land, and discover how the wind affects flight. With time and practice and their parents' encouragement, this all becomes natural and they can take with full ease to the air.

All in all birds are committed parents, guardians and teachers and, as with humans, they like to be with their fellows. More, pairing can, it seems, be a deep commitment and, apparently, joy, sometimes for life. Further different species, deeply imbued with their looking-out-for-others social outlook sometimes join up in caring for each other, for example a red rosella tenderly grooming its cockatiel companion (photo at Barber 1994 p.114).

Of course, not all is sweetness and harmony. Birds also *fight* – yet another aspect of the social nature of avian life in the sense of an awareness of competition, of threats, of the need for self-defence.

They fight over food or to protect their territory. They organise a coordinated foray against an enemy (sometimes, specially with corvids, one remembered fur an offence years ago) with many individuals joining in the coordinated group action made possible by their socially shared living.

And then there Is the spectacular and mysterious phenomenon of joint "flocking" when hundreds or thousands of birds fly together, each individually and yet as if one organism: well in one sense it *is* a single organism. We understand very little of how this works: of how birds can be so in touch and communicating and coordinating that with no hold-up for looking and listening, they move together as one.

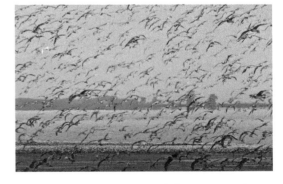

We can speculate however (that after all is a human habit). We are accustomed for example to think of twins as sharing some kind of extrasensory non–physical contact even from a distance. So it would not be surprising if bird siblings had the same kind of communicating both during flocking and at other times, and then maybe the cousins and the other close relatives too going back many generations. Perhaps we do not after all have to seek for other explanations for the mystery of flocking.

Another interesting indicator of forms of communication beyond what human beings are, at least consciously capable of, comes from a familiar setting. Blue tits love the cream that forms just under the tops of the bottles of milk once left daily on people's doorsteps. *One* bird – accident or design we don't know – pecked through the foil top to reach the delectable nectar below. Within days all the blue tits throughout the country and beyond were doing the same thing. By what magic communication did they achieve this? Is this the same wondrous contact as that by which a flock of birds swerves and sweeps together.

And have we not perhaps observed the same thing with a company of matching men – both one and many – a choir, a prayer group, yoga class, enraged or panicking crowd?

An important recent move has been the development of "swarm studies", stimulated by the study of bird flocking. This has drawn attention – and analysis – to how a flock can move in perfect coordination *not* because an individual sees or hears its fellow's movement (that would make them separate, and apart from/ behind the group) but because the togetherness as of a single organism lets them swoop and fly as one (on swarm studies and the parallels with insect swarming, fish schooling, choir singing, and robots, *see* https://en.wikipedia.org/wiki/Swarm behaviour/ *and* Hayward 2019).

Hopefully we will understand and learn more as the years go by, no doubt with the help of birds.

Day to day

All through their lives, the central preoccupation of birds – as individuals, as parents, pairs, groups – is, and has it be, the locating and seizing of food pin either established, local, migratory, or (typical of birds) new and opportunistic ways. Linked to this, location and species are both important factors in determining what food a bird eats. The location contributes to the types of food sources available, whilst the species of bird creates a variance in diet due to differences in size, strength, ability and needs.

Birds between them eat a huge variety of things: beetles, flies, spiders, earthworms, rotting fish, offal, poison oak berries, weed seeds, and so on. Not only that, most birds have diets that are quite monotonous – some passerines subsist for weeks mainly on grasshoppers, brants dine near-exclusively on eelgrass, and snail kites almost nothing but snails. In spite of this, the nutritional requirements of birds are not very different from ours; they need proteins, fats, carbohydrates, vitamins, and minerals.

Carbohydrates and fats are primarily energy sources, but proteins – more specifically the nitrogen-containing amino acids that are the building blocks of proteins – are needed for construction of tissues, enzymes, and so on. Reproduction, growth, and moulting all need more nitrogen than simple maintenance of the body, and proteins are the source of that nitrogen.

It is no surprise therefore that omnivorous birds (eating both plant and animal food) such as red-winged blackbirds up their proportion of protein-rich animal food in the breeding season. Many herbivorous birds such as sparrows subsist for much of the year on a relatively low-protein vegetable diet, but in the breeding season eat as many insects as they can, and often provide their young with a diet comprised entirely of insects. Similarly, wood warblers, which are considered carnivorous feed themselves and their young virtually exclusively on insects in the breeding season while berries and other plant foods are a substantial portion of their fall / winter intake. And nectarivores, such as hummingbirds, catch insects to provide protein to balance their energy-rich but nitrogen-poor intake of nectar when breeding.

It is, of course, no miracle that protein–rich food sources just happen to be more abundant during the breeding season. Just the reverse – evolution has timed the breeding season so that it occurs when the needed nitrogen can be obtained.

Birds' mineral requirements are much like ours. Calcium, needed in large quantities for egg production, is a critical mineral nutrient for reproductively active female birds. It is thought that shortage of calcium may restrict the reproductive output of vultures, which devour only the soft, calcium-poor parts of carcasses. This may be the reason that some vultures supplement their diets with small vertebrate prey that can be swallowed whole.

This is *my* territory

And then there is territoriality, an important part of ensuring food resources and a further acknowledgement of the existence – and potential threat – of others: a significant aspect again of birds' *social* existence.

A home range is anywhere a bird happens to wander – basically anywhere in its appropriate habitat. A *territory* however is a defended area within that home range and is typical of songbirds but also found among a number of other birds. A territory may be held by one bird, a pair, or a flock. It may be held for all or only part of a year. It may be very large such as those held by eagles and provide all the resources the bird needs or only a part or be very small such as nesting territories of cliff birds like kittiwakes. It may be vigorously defended or loosely guarded. Depending on the abundance of the resources, it might be closely held one year and not at all the next. Territories are typically asserted against others of the same species but it can also be against other species,

A territory is what a bird defends against others because it contains resources that are in short supply, so the greater the population size the greater the competition for resources. A lot of competition requires a lot of aggressiveness. But if it costs too much then territories are not held.

The level of aggression birds show in defence of their territory varies depending on the species and their interaction with one another. An American robin, for example, will chase away other robins from its territory, but it won't mind a white-breasted nuthatch sharing the same space because they do not compete for food sources or bother each other.

Northern mockingbird territorial display

Migratory birds begin to claim territory in late winter or early spring as mature males arrive from their wintering grounds and seek for the best places to attract a mate. Non-migratory birds also renew their claims on territory at this time, in part to attract their mates and renew bonds but also to let arriving migrants know that the territory is already spoken for.

Birds claim their territory in several ways.

Singing is one of the commonest ways that birds advertise that territory belongs to them. Songs carry quite far, and birds perch near the edge of their territory to broadcast their claim to the maximum range. At the same time, a strong, vibrant song can help to attract a mate. For some species, such as the northern mockingbird, more complex songs help birds defend a larger territory and are more attractive to females. Skylarks advertise their territories by a spectacular song-flight, during which the bird rises almost vertically with rapid wing-beats, hovering for several minutes and then parachuting down. Song flights of up to one hour have been recorded, and the birds can reach 1,000 feet before descending.

Nest building: Some birds, for example wrens, claim territory by taking advantage of the nesting sites it offers. The males build multiple nests in suitable locations throughout their territory, females investigate the nests and choose the one they prefer, even if they eventually rebuild the male's construction to suit their preferences.

Drumming: Woodpeckers and several types of game birds claim territory by drumming, an alternative to singing. These low-pitched, rhythmic sounds, whether made by pounding on a hollow tree or by using air sacs, carry great distances. This alerts competing birds that the territory is not available, as well as telling potential mates that a strong, healthy bird has claimed the location.

Visual displays such as puffing up collared feather patches, tail flicking, or fanning and wing spreading are all part of claiming territory. These postures and actions also show off a bird's strength and health to a potential mate.

Chasing: As a last resort, aggressive birds directly chase intruders or competitors out of their territory. This is frequent in areas where many birds are seeking to claim the same space, or when a dominant male is discouraging younger males that are struggling to claim their first territory. In bird species where family groups remain together in the winter, the male parent may chase away his mature offspring the following spring so they do not infringe on his territory.

Most birds use a combination of these strategies to claim and defend their territories.

Some species however, such as communal nesting birds. are not territorial at all. Swifts, swallows, herons, and many waterfowl are colonial nesters and have only very small territories directly around the nest site that they defend, with the larger area shared by all nesting birds.

Birds are less territorial after the breeding season ends. By then birds that would earlier have been aggressively defending their space are gathering together for migration. Even non–migratory birds are less aggressive at this time since competition is easing for food sources and they no longer have to meet the demands of growing chicks.

Territoriality, then, provokes visual and vocal displays and movement. It is not without some risks of course. The individual exposes itself to aggression from other birds and predators, but on the other hand there are the benefits from improved exploitation of resources, and lowered diseases and predation rates. For example, Brewer's blackbird nests are preyed upon more frequently when the nests are closer together – territories serve to spread them apart. In the case of colonial nesters, such as egrets, swallows, and many seabirds, the individual territories are small but the colony is large and serves to deter predators.

Different species have different sized territories. Most garden birds have quite small territories, from a few square yards (house sparrows for instance) up to an acre or so (blackbirds) while those of birds of prey like eagles and buzzards can be many square miles. Wild birds need the best possible territory for feeding, mating, and raising young, and claim it in a variety of ways, choosing it because there they can meet their needs for food, water, shelter, and nesting.

Breeding territories average about an acre in size, while winter territories are around half of this. The exact size depends on the quality of habitat and the density of birds in the area.

The size of the territory thus varies by species and their needs, including how sociable the birds are. Some species need large territories with little competition, while others have more communal needs and are more apt to share territory with larger flocks.

The size of a bird's territory can also vary from year to year depending on how viable and productive the land is. In a year when there are excellent food sources, for example, a bird may claim less territory than in years when food is scarce

Most territories tend to be more or less circular but the shape varies. Stream bank feeders such as the kingfisher have linear territories. Birds that feed on animal food have larger territories than those that feed on plant food. So there are maximum and minimum sizes of territories, the maximum size being controlled by defensibility and the minimum by density of resources.

In some areas (such as Scottish pinewoods with well-spaced, mature trees and few shrubs) breeding densities can be as low as 10 pairs per a third of a square, while a lowland woodland can support as many as 200-300 pairs in that area, but territorial boundaries are fluid, and change frequently as circumstances change.

The amount of aggressiveness in defence of the territory also varies. It may be more advantageous to strongly defend a high-quality territory than weakly defend a poor one.

Robins are among the few birds to hold a territory all year round. In summer their territory is defended by a mated pair, while each bird holds individual winter territories. The purpose of a robin's red breast is in territory defence rather than for courtship. A patch of red triggers territorial behaviour, and robins are known to persistently attack stuffed robins and even tufts of red feathers.

Territoriality among the same species is the most common. As a rule, birds of one species will tolerate birds of other species in their territories and chase out only conspecifics. A bald eagle and a great horned owl, for example. nested in the same tree in Florida only one meter apart. Swallows often nest in eagle and hawk nests. Birds chase other birds out of their territories if they are potential competitors or predators. Oystercatchers, for example, chase gulls, ravens, and crows from their territories.

Territories obviously affect the social system of birds. The male fiery-throated hummingbird of Costa Rica and Panama holds a territory; a female is attracted to the flowers in that territory, but feeds on different flowers from the males. The female selects the territories on the basis of the best food source.

So territoriality is, for many birds, part of their predictable and in a sense dependable culture, involving defence and self-assertion and indeed sometimes fighting, one aspect, as with humans, of being social beings, interacting and competing with others.

Migrating, venturing, navigating

A coordinated flock of birds flying purposefully together? what you are seeing is a case of bird migration, one of the wonders of the natural world. It is an example, and a of the regular seasonal movements made so remarkably by animals from one part of the world to another and back again.

Animal movement, including that of birds, is, generally speaking, linked to fundamental ecological and evolutionary processes. Like other animals, birds migrate to survive and to cope with the risks and needs they face in their daily lives, driven mostly by weather, temperature, and the availability of food – yet another mark of birds' ability to adapt to conditions. For individual birds, migration facilitates access to spatially and temporally varying resources. They travel to find better resources and to survive, as all over the world, every year, millions of them are so impressively on the move.

There are, it is true, costs and challenges associated with migration. The most serious is navigation – the birds must somehow find their way through often complex environments along migration routes that can cover tens of thousands of miles and take months to traverse (can humans do this?). To successfully complete these travels, they employ a diverse range of sensory modalities and an impressive range of cues, including celestial cues from the sun and stars, the earth's magnetic field, and mental maps. While in some contexts the preferred navigation route is genetically encoded and instinctive, in others it must be discovered or learned from others.

Migration carries high costs in predation and mortality, including from hunting by humans, and is driven primarily by availability of food. It occurs mainly in the northern hemisphere, where birds are funnelled onto specific routes by natural barriers such as the Mediterranean Sea or the Caribbean Sea.

Not all birds fly across the globe, but for those who do the range can be staggering. Arctic terns travel between Arctic breeding grounds and the Antarctic each year, while manx shearwaters and others travel over eight thousand miles every year between their northern breeding grounds and the southern ocean.

Shorter migrations are common too, including altitudinal migrations (moving to a different height level) on mountains ranges like the Andes and Himalayas. In the tropics there is little variation in the length of day throughout the year, and it is always warm enough for a food supply so long-distance migration may not be needed in the same way, but some tropical birds practise altitudinal migration so they can obtain more of their preferred foods such as fruits at a different height.

The world is criss-crossed with bird migration routes. In Asia, many northern species spend winter in the tropical south-east, with some, like spine-tailed swifts, getting as far as Australia by flying down through the islands of Indonesia. In America, birds from the northern USA and Canada migrate to South and Central America. America has no seas or deserts to separate the north from the south, so migration is easier for birds that need to feed along the way, making it possible for tropical species from South America like the ruby-throated hummingbird to extend their breeding range as far north as Canada. Not all birds fly south for the winter: some that breed in the southern hemisphere migrate north to find a winter home with more food and warmth.

Yes, all over the world, and in every year, millions of birds in their way. The scale is near unimaginable. In one case of pigeon migration for example the enormous flocks were a mile wide, darkening the sky, and hundreds of miles long, taking several days to pass. Common species, such as the *European honey buzzard can be counted in hundreds of thousands in the* autumn. *Some* birds visit *well over twenty countries on their annual journey of many thousands of miles. Migration from one part of the world to another and back again is, in short, truly amazing.*

Minoan fresco of swallows gathering in springtime at Akrotiri, c. 1500 BC

The incredible journey and its history

Bird migrations were recorded in Europe from millennia ago by ancient Greek writers like Hesiod, *Homer*, Herodotus and Aristotle. The Bible, as in the Book of Job, notes migrations with the inquiry: "Is it by your insight that the hawk hovers, spreads its wings southward?" The author of Jeremiah wrote: "Even the stork in the heavens know its seasons, and the turtle dove, the swift and the crane keep the time of their arrival".

In the Pacific, traditional land-finding techniques used by the Micronesians and Polynesians suggest that bird migration was observed and interpreted for more than 3000 years. In

Samoan island tradition, Tagaloa sent his daughter Sina to Earth in the form of a bird, Tuli, to find dry land, the word tuli referring specifically to land-finding waders, often to the Pacific golden plover.

But it was not until the end of the eighteenth century that migration (rather than hibernation) was accepted as the explanation for the winter disappearance of birds from northern climes. As always, the history of science was fuelled by personal observations and discoveries.

Thomas Bewick in his *A History of British Birds* in 1797 mentions "a very intelligent master of a vessel" who, "between the islands of Menorca and Majorca, saw great numbers of Swallows flying northward" and concludes that "Swallows do not in any material instance differ from other birds in their nature and propensies [for life in the air] … they leave us when this country can no longer furnish them with a supply of their proper and natural food".

Then in 1822, a white stork was found in the German state of Mecklenburg with a dateable arrow made from central African hardwood, which provided some of the earliest evidence of long-distance stork migration.

General patterns of migration

Migration, then, a common avian practice, is the regular seasonal movement, often between north and south, undertaken by many species of birds, usually in response to differences or changes in food availability, habitat, or weather. Sometimes, journeys are not termed "true migration" because they are irregular (nomadism, invasions, irruptions) or in only one direction (dispersal, movement of young away from natal area). Migration proper is marked by its annual seasonality.

Approximately 1800 of the world's 10-11,000 bird species migrate long distances along an established flyway. The most common pattern involves flying north in the spring to breed in the temperate summer and returning in the autumn to wintering grounds in warmer regions to the south. In the southern hemisphere the directions are reversed, but there is less land area in the far south to support long-distance migration so bird migration is primarily (but not entirely) a northern hemisphere phenomenon: the continental landmasses of the northern

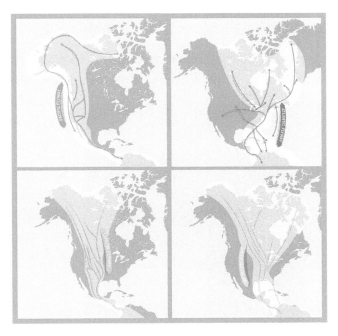

The map shows the flightways of North and Central America: Pacific, Atlantic, Central and Mississipi Source:perkypet.com

The Rostocker Pfeilstorch demonstrated that birds migrated rather than hibernating or changing form in winter

hemisphere are subject to winter food shortages driving bird populations south to overwinter. The primary physiological cue for migration is changes in day length, related to hormonal changes in the birds. In the period before migration, many birds display higher activity as well as physiological changes such as increased fat deposition.

Thus, the typical pattern of migration is of northern land birds like swallows and birds of prey making long flights to the tropics.

However, many arctic wildfowl and *finch* species winter in the north temperate zone in regions with milder winters than their summer breeding grounds. For example, wild geese migrate from *Iceland* to Britain and neighbouring countries, whilst the dark-eyed junco migrates from subarctic and arctic climates to the contiguous United States, and the American goldfinch from taiga to wintering grounds extending from the American South northwestward to *Western Oregon*. Some wild ducks move completely or partially into the tropics. The European pied flycatcher follows this migratory trend, breeding in Asia and Europe and wintering in Africa.

Birds fly at varying altitudes during migration. An expedition to Mount Everest found skeletons of northern pintail and black-tailed godwit at 16,000 ft on the Khumbu Glacier. Bar-headed geese have been recorded by GPS flying at 6,000 yards up while crossing the Himalayas, at the same time engaging in the highest rates of climb to altitude for any bird. Seabirds fly low over water but higher when crossing land, whereas land birds do the opposite. Most collisions occur below 2,000 ft. and almost none above (6,000 ft).

Migrating is not limited to birds that can fly. Emus in *Australia* undertake long-distance movements on foot during droughts. Some species of penguin migrate by swimming, others

by walking, Little is known about how penguins find their way during migration, but the travels of the emperor penguins are legendary.

Migration routes and wintering grounds seem to be both genetically and traditionally determined depending on the social system of the species. In long-lived species like white storks flocks are led by the oldest members and young storks learn the route on their first journey.

In shorter-lived species that migrate alone, such as Eurasian blackcaps or yellow-billed cuckoos, first-year migrants follow an apparently genetically determined route (alterable with selective breeding).

The primary motivation for migration is food. For example, some hummingbirds choose not to migrate if fed through the winter. In addition, the longer days of the northern summer provide extended time for breeding birds to feed their young. This helps diurnal birds to produce larger clutches than related non-migratory species that remain in the tropics. As the days shorten in autumn, the birds return to warmer regions where the available food supply varies little with the season. These advantages offset the high stress, physical exertion costs, and other risks of the migration, such as heightened predation at that time. The higher concentrations of migrating birds at stopover sites also make them more prone to parasites and pathogens, which require a heightened immune response.

The Arctic tern has the furthest migration of any bird, and sees more daylight than any other, moving from its Arctic breeding grounds to the Antarctic non-breeding areas. One arctic tern, ringed as a chick on the Farne Islands off the British east coast, reached Melbourne, *Australia* in just three months from fledging, a journey of around 14,000 miles. Most seabird species are great wanderers, and the *albatrosses* of the southern oceans circle the globe as they ride the "roaring forties" outside the breeding season. The tubenoses spread widely over large areas of open ocean, but congregate when food becomes available. Many are  among the longest-distance migrants; shear waters nesting on the Falkland Islands *migrate* over 8,000 miles between the breeding colony and the North Atlantic Ocean off Norway. As they are long-lived birds, they cover enormous distances during their lives; one record-breaking manx shearwater is calculated to have flown 5 million miles during its 50+ years of life.

Within a given species, not all populations may be migratory. This is common in the southern continents; in Australia, 44% of non-passerine birds and 32% of passerine species are only partially migratory. In some species, the population at higher latitudes tends to be migratory, wintering at lower latitudes. The migrating birds bypass the latitudes where other populations are sedentary and suitable wintering habitats already occupied. Many fully migratory species follow this leap-frog migration pattern, and some the alternative, chain migration, where populations "slide" more evenly north and south without reversing. Within a population too, different ages and/or sexes may have different patterns of timing and distance: female *chaffinches in Eastern Fennoscandia* for example migrate earlier in the autumn than males.

How do they get there?

Birds travel thousands of miles every year, and arrive. How?

One thing is the choice of appropriate routes. Migrating birds do not just point themselves in the right direction and hope for the best. Each species has its traditional route, pioneered by we know not which venturesome bird or birds in the far distant past and now (human-like) adopted into the culture of the following generations.

Most routes follow obvious landmarks such as river valleys or coastlines. Some birds take winding routes around the coast, others travel more directly, even if this means crossing perilous stretches of desert or sea. Routes often converge at certain junctions, such as mountain passes or narrow sea crossings. Many migrating birds return along roughly the same, known, route as the outward journey, others a different way, in a roughly circular journey.

This "loop migration" means birds can access the best food supplies or weather patterns in different places at different times.

The Mediterranean Sea is a massive barrier for birds flying between Europe and Africa, one they have to negotiate in one way or another. Some small birds, with enough energy to keep flapping, cross wherever they can but many larger birds head for the narrowest crossing points, some going west via Gibraltar where the straits are narrowest, others reaching Africa through Turkey and Israel. In spring and autumn, thousands of storks, kites and other large birds gather at these points, waiting for thermals – which only form over land – to lift them up high enough, then the wind to carry them over the sea.

And then there is the huge barrier of the Sahara Desert between Europe and tropical Africa. More than 500 million birds have to cross it twice a year. Wading birds like dunlins avoid it by flying down the coast, feeding at estuaries along the way but many land birds, such as cuckoos, cross in one non-stop flight. When they reach the other side, they land, exhausted, in the first green space they find, feeding to gain the energy for the final leg.

Mountain ranges *and other barriers can cause funnelling, particularly of large diurnal migrants, as in the* Central American *migratory bottleneck. The Batumi bottleneck in the Caucasus is one of the heaviest migratory funnels on earth, created when hundreds of thousands of soaring birds avoid flying over the Black Sea and across high mountains.*

So the migration routes of a long-distance migratory birds often don't follow a straight line between breeding and wintering grounds but a hooked or arched way, with detours around geographical barriers or towards suitable stopovers. For most land birds, the barriers are large stretches of water or high mountain ranges, a lack of stopover or feeding sites, or a lack of thermal columns (important for broad-winged birds).

Additionally, many migration routes are circuitous due to evolutionary history. For example, the breeding range of northern wheatears can now cover the entire northern hemisphere, but the species still migrates up 9,000 miles to reach ancestral wintering grounds in sub-Saharan Africa rather than establish new wintering grounds closer to their breeding areas.

The same considerations about barriers and detours as for long-distance land birds also apply to water birds, but in reverse: a large area of land without water to offer feeding sites is a barrier for these birds, So, brent geese migrating from the Taymyr Peninsula to the Wadden Sea travel via the White Sea coast and the Baltic Sea rather than flying directly across the Arctic Ocean and northern *Scandinavia*. Bar-tailed godwit waders are the same, while others like the semipalmated sandpipers go longer distances to reach the Southern Hemisphere tropics.

For some species of waders, migration success depends on the availability of key food resources at stopover points along the migration route so the birds can refuel for the next leg of the journey. Some examples of important stopover locations are the Bay of Fundy that lies between Canada's Nova Scotia and New Brunswick provinces, and Delaware Bay on the northeast seaboard of the United States. Approximately 782 square miles in area, the bay's fresh water mixes for many miles with the salt water of the Atlantic Ocean.

Most migrations begin with the birds starting off in a broad front which often then narrows into one or more preferred routes (flyways). These typically follow mountain ranges or coastlines, sometimes rivers, and where possible take advantage of updrafts and other wind patterns, and avoid geographical barriers such as large stretches of open water.

Birds are physically adapted to long flights where food is likely to be unavailable or at least scarce, with a good proportion of their bodyweight stored as fat, Thus, with bar-tailed godwits, who have the longest known non-stop flight of any migrant, flying 9,000 miles from Alaska to *New Zealand*, 55 percent of their bodyweight is stored as fat which fuels this uninterrupted journey.

Most birds migrate in flocks. For larger birds in particular, flying in flocks reduces the energy cost. Geese in a V-formation may conserve 12-20% of the energy they would need to fly alone. Red knots and dunlins were found in radar studies to fly 3.1 mph faster in flocks than when they were flying alone

In the springtime, many birds gather together ready to set off to temperate regions, where food is plentiful and they can safely create nests – flying together on routes known to the experienced is safest. In the autumn, they do the same ready to move to warmer latitudes, following their food sources and more comfortable weather patterns. Long-distance migrants are believed to disperse as young birds and form attachments to both potential breeding sites and favourite wintering sites. Once the site attachment is made they show high site-fidelity, visiting the same familiar wintering sites year after year.

It helps if they go in an organised flock, both so that the experienced can guide the youngsters on the route and because – as with a column of marching men – this conserves energy.

Though there are some startling instances of single birds flying thousands of miles on their own, birds do best if they keep together. They need to avoid collisions however, specially in the dark. During nocturnal migration, many birds give special flight calls: short contact measures that maintain the composition of a migrating flock, and avoid collisions. Nocturnal migrants land in the morning and often feed for a few days before resuming their migration, as "passage migrants" in the regions where they occur for a short period between the origin and destination. Nocturnal migrants minimise depredation, avoid overheating, and can feed during the day.

Flocks of birds assembling before migration southwards

Many long–distance migrants appear to be programmed to respond to changing day length. Species that move short distances, however, may not need such a timing mechanism, instead moving in response to local weather conditions. Thus, mountain and moorland breeders, such as wallcreeper and white-throated dipper may move only altitudinally to escape the cold higher ground. Others such as merlins and Eurasian skylarks move further, to the coast or towards the south. Species like the chaffinch are less migratory in Britain than those of continental Europe, mostly not moving more than 3 or 4 miles in their lives.

Many bird species across southern Australia are nomadic: they follow water and food supply around the country in an irregular pattern, unrelated to season but related to rainfall. Several years may pass between visits to an area by a particular species.

Sometimes circumstances such as a good breeding season followed by a food source failure the following year, lead to irruptions in which large numbers of a species move far beyond the normal range. Bohemian waxwings showed this unpredictable variation in annual numbers, with five major arrivals in Britain during the nineteenth century, but 18 between the years 1937 and 2000. Red crossbills too have had widespread invasions across England, noted in 1251, 1593, 1757, and 1791.

Birds have to alter their metabolism to meet the demands of migration. The storage of energy through the accumulation of fat and the control of sleep in nocturnal migrants require special physiological adaptations. In addition, the feathers of a bird suffer from wear-and-tear and need to be moulted.

The timing of this moult – usually once a year but sometimes twice – varies: some species moult before moving to their winter grounds and others before returning to their breeding grounds. Apart from physiological adaptations, migration sometimes requires behavioural changes such as flying in flocks to reduce the energy needed and the risk of predators who try to take advantage of the concentration of birds during migration.

Large scale climatic changes are expected to have an effect on the timing of migration. Studies have shown a variety of effects including timing changes in migration, breeding and population declines. Many species have been expanding their range, sometimes in the form of former vagrants becoming established or regular migrants. The concentration of birds during migration can also put them at risk. Some spectacular migrants have already gone extinct and hunting along migration routes threatens some bird species, such as Siberian cranes in Central Asia.

Mediaeval sketch by Matthew Paris in his Chronica Majora (1251) recording that year's major irruption of red crossbills into England

Human activities too have threatened many migratory bird species. Power lines, wind farms and offshore oil-rigs can affect migratory birds, together with pollution, wildfires, and habitat destruction along migration routes, denying migrants food at stopover points. Many historic sites have been destroyed or drastically reduced by human agricultural development. The distances involved in bird migration mean that they often cross political boundaries of countries and conservation measures require international cooperation (by now several international treaties have been signed to protect migratory species).

Navigating

Navigating is an amazing feature of bird migration. How – no compasses, no maps, no technological navigation aids – how do they find their way across these many thousands of miles?

Scientists are still not entirely sure how birds do it, but most likely they use a combination of techniques. One idea, suggested by Charles Darwin back in 1873, is that they use dead reckoning, i.e. calculate where they are by the distance made from their known starting point, based on their speed and direction. More recently the focus has been on navigation by the polarisation pattern of the blue sky, by the earth's magnetic field and, especially and wherever possible, by the sun.

The manx shearwater is one of the most thoroughly studied. Living on the remote island of Skokholm. These small seabirds make one of the longest migrations of any bird over 6000 miles – but return to the exact same nesting burrow on Skokholm year after year. It can orient itself and fly home at full speed when released far away so long as either the sun or the stars are visible.

Homing pigeons are an interesting and familiar example, a variety of domestic pigeons derived from the wild rock dove (which has an innate homing ability) selectively bred for their ability to find their way home over extremely long distances.

But overall bird navigating along routes sometimes many thousands of miles longboard is still a puzzle *to scientists*. One theory is that the birds are able to detect a magnetic field to help them find their way home. Other suggestions are the influence of a light-mediated mechanism, by low-frequency infrasound, or by atmospheric odours – olfactory navigation. GPS (global positioning system) tracing studies indicate that gravitational anomalies may also play a role. Other research indicates that homing pigeons also navigate through visual landmarks by following familiar roads and other man-made features, making 90-degree turns and following habitual routes in much the same way that humans navigate.

Various experiments suggest that different breeds of homing pigeons rely selectively on different cues; while pigeons from one loft were confused by a magnetic anomaly in the earth this had no effect on birds from another loft a mile away. Other experiments have shown that altering the perceived time of day with artificial lighting or using air conditioning to eliminate odours in the pigeons' home roost affected their' ability to return home.

One probability is that they have an internal GPS that allows them to follow the same pattern every year. A young bird imprints on the sun and stars to help orient it. Some researchers think a bird may also recognise landmarks.

Individual organs also contribute to a bird's remarkable navigational ability. A bird's eyes interact with its brain in a region called "cluster N", which probably helps the bird determine which way is north. Tiny amounts of iron in the neurons of a bird's inner ear also help.

Surprisingly, a bird's beak helps navigation by helping birds determine their exact position. The trigeminal nerve, which connects a bird's beak to its brain, may also help a bird assess its exact location. Researchers think this nerve helps birds evaluate the strength of the earth's magnetic field, which is stronger at the poles and weaker at the equator. Birds may also be able to *smell* their way, using an olfactory map to orient them to terrain and topography.

Some large broad-winged birds rely on thermal columns of rising hot air to enable them to soar as they go; some even, apparently, sleep on the wing.

Griffon vulture soaring

These include birds of prey such as vultures, *eagles*, and *buzzards*, but also storks, who migrate in the daytime. Migratory species in these groups have great difficulty crossing large bodies of water, since thermals only form over land, and these birds cannot maintain active flight for long distances. *Mediterranean* and other seas present a major obstacle to soaring birds too, who must cross at the narrowest points.

Massive numbers of large raptors and storks pass through areas such as the Strait of Messina, Gibraltar, *Falsterbo*, and the Bosphorus at migration times. Birds of prey like honey buzzards who use thermals lose only 10 to 20% of their weight during migration, which may explain why they forage less during migration than smaller birds of prey with more active flight such as falcons, hawks and harriers.

The ability of birds to navigate during migrations cannot be fully explained by endogenous programming, even with the help of responses to environmental cues. The ability to successfully perform long-distance migrations can probably only be fully explained by taking account of birds' cognitive ability in recognising habitats and forming mental maps.

Birds thus probably rely on a combination of innate biological senses, experience, and leadership by more experienced birds. A young bird on its first migration flies in the correct direction according to the earth's magnetic field, but does not know how far the journey will be. At this stage the bird is somewhat in the position of a Boy Scout with a compass but no map, until it grows accustomed to the journey and can put its other capabilities to use. With experience it learns the landmarks and this "mapping" may be done by magnetites in the trigeminal system that tell the bird how strong the field is. Because birds migrate between northern and southern regions, the magnetic field strengths at different latitudes let it know when they have reached their destination. There is a neural connection between the eye and "Cluster N", the part of the forebrain that is active during migrational orientation, suggesting that birds may actually be able to *see* the magnetic field of the earth.

All in all, scientists now think, birds' remarkable skill in finding their way is based on a variety of senses and a combination of abilities, especially the ability to detect magnetic fields (magnetoreception), visual landmarks, and olfactory cues. The birds that *use a sun compass* also have to be able to calculate adjustments based on time.

Migrating birds do sometimes lose their way and appear outside their normal ranges. They may, for example, have flown past their destinations as in the "spring overshoot" in which birds returning to their breeding areas end up further north than intended. Certain areas, because of their location, have become famous as watchpoints for such birds. Reverse migration, where the genetic programming of young birds fails to work properly, can lead to rarities turning up as vagrants thousands of miles out of their way. Or – drift migration – they may have been blown off course by the wind resulting in "falls" of large numbers of migrants at coastal sites. There is also "abmigration" where birds from one region join similar birds from a different breeding region in their common winter grounds and then migrate back along with the new population (frequent among some waterfowl) – a shift from one flyway to another. Building on this, it has been possible to teach a new migration route to a flock of birds, for example in re-introduction schemes.

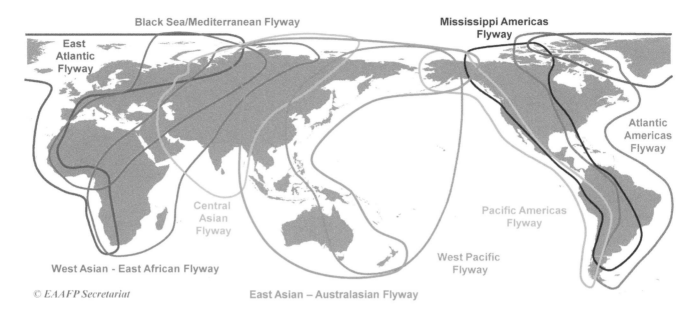

East Asian—Australasian Flyway
Map and copy below from the Department of Environment and Science, Queensland
WetlandInfo website, accessed 26 Nov. 2021

The East Asian-Australasian Flyway includes a complex of islands and ocean crossings, spans many countries and contains nearly half the world's humans. Areas of the Flyway are subject to large-scale, rapid economic development and consequently many waterbird populations in this flyway are threatened or in decline. Migratory shorebirds breed in parts of northeast Asia (eastern Siberia and China), to as far west as the Taymyr Peninsula in the far north of Russia and as far east as Alaska (e.g. some bar-tailed godwits). Most of these birds migrate southward before the onset of winter, with the destination for many being the warmer feeding habitats of Australia.

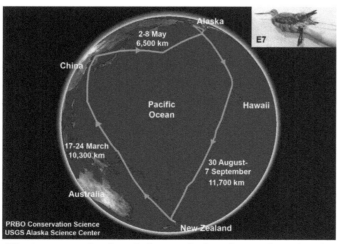

The journey of a female bar-tailed godwit referred to by researchers as 'E7'

After spending the summer in the south, the first leg of the northward migration from Australia for waterbirds can be a very long flight of more than 6,000 km to reach a staging site in the flyway, such as the mudflats around the Yellow Sea in China and Korea. The Yellow Sea region of the flyway is especially important as birds need to spend time here feeding to regain weight lost in consuming body fat that powered the first leg of their journey north from Australia, and to prepare for arrival at their breeding grounds.

Many possible mechanisms, therefore, have been suggested. The main current ones can be summarised as follows, each with at least *some* evidence to support them:

Remembered landmarks

Birds are clearly capable of learning and remembering these.

Orientation by the sun

An important cross-species mechanism

Orientation by the night sky

To use this – i.e. to navigate by the stars – birds would need both a built-in ability to read patterns of stars and to navigate by them, which also requires an accurate time-of-day clock.

Orientation by polarised light

This works for bees, why not for birds?

Magnetoreception

Birds such as pigeons are apparently sensitive to the earth's magnetic field. Homing pigeons use magnetic field information with other navigational cues. Time-shifted homing pigeons could not orient themselves correctly on a clear sunny day, but could do so on an overcast day, suggesting that the birds prefer to rely on the direction of the sun, but switch to using a magnetic field cue when the sun is not visible. This was confirmed by experiments with magnets: the pigeons could not orient correctly on an overcast day when the magnetic field was disrupted.

Olfaction

Navigation using smell has been suggested as a possible mechanism, taking it that the birds build a mental map of the odours in their area, recognising where they are by the local odour. There is some evidence that pigeons unable to detect odours are less able to orient and navigate than normal pigeons, so smell does seem to be important in pigeon navigation though it is not clear how the cues are used.

Gravity receptors

Possible though as yet little understood.

Way-marking

This relies on reckoning the distance and direction travelled from a start point to estimate current position, putting together cues from different sensory sources within the body, without reference to *visual* or other external landmarks, to estimate position relative to a known starting point continuously while travelling on a path that is not necessarily straight.

Little by little, or trial and error

Older more experienced birds, remembering the routes, guide the younger ones. But that leaves the question of how that knowledge was gained in the first place. Given the millions of years of bird development one possibility is of increasingly long exploratory flights by adventurous pioneers from the initial, known, environment, over gradually widening learned pathways so that by the end routes of thousands of miles would have been learned, assisted no doubt by the any or all of the mechanisms listed above. The consequent collective navigation would result in individuals improving their ability to find their way – one of the key benefits of sociality – leading to the accumulation of knowledge at the group level and the establishing of learned migratory culture.

Although the mechanisms of animal navigation have fascinated researchers for decades, an interesting point is that they have *primarily* focused on the level of the individual. However, many migratory species are known to move in large groups and social interactions can alter migratory movement decisions and affect, most likely improve, individual navigational ability.

Thus, *flocks* may be better than individuals at locating thermal updrafts along their migration route, which the birds use to gain altitude more efficiently. Collective learning can lead to the emergence and retention of new knowledge resulting from the dynamics of social interactions. It can also provide opportunities for inexperienced individuals to learn migratory routes and other relevant information for use in future journeys.

Cumulative culture is frequently claimed to be a human-unique trait absent from other species through necessitating a suite of sophisticated socio-cognitive functions the combination of which only humans are argued to possess. But studies of, for example, pigeon groups seem to show that knowledge about increasingly better travel routes was *accumulate*d through collective learning, and was passed on both between individuals in groups and across generations through social learning.

Collective navigation applies not only to large-scale orientational tasks such as migrations but also to a wide range of other behavioural contexts. Navigation is important for locating new sources of food, seeking new shelters or any other task where animals must use environmental information to make decisions about where to go.

For birds, as most likely for the different context for human navigating and exploring, there are thus many cues and markers, depending on the species, the environment, the time of year and no doubt cultural assumptions and knowledge. Often a crucial factor seems to be that the birds – social beings – fly in a group, both more energy efficient and a context where the experienced old hands lead the younger ones. Finally, all of these biological systems may yield mechanisms, "discovered" during eons of evolution, that provide lessons and inspiration for human technologies such as swarm robotics and particle swarm optimisation.

Flying messengers

Bird-human collaboration has a long history based on this ability of birds to find their way, unerringly and fast, over vast distances. Pigeons are especially notable, with flights as long as 1,100 miles recorded in competitive pigeon racing with an average flying speed over moderate (600 miles) distances at around 60 mph per hour and up to too racers' 100 mph over shorter distances. Because of this skill, domesticated pigeons have often been used to carry messages as messenger pigeons: "pigeon post" if used in post service, or "war pigeon" during wars. Until the introduction of telephones, homing pigeons were commonly used commercially to deliver communication.

But there had been many years of bird-human collaboration before that. In 3000 BC, Egypt was using homing pigeons for pigeon post, taking advantage of a bird's capacity, even when taken far from its nest, to find its way home. Messages were tied round the pigeon's legs which, when freed, could reach its original nest.

Pigeons were used in the fifth century BC to proclaim the winner of the ancient Greek Olympic Games while by 1167 a regular pigeon service between Baghdad and Syria had been established by Sultan Nur ad-Din. In *Damietta*, by the mouth of the Nile, the Spanish traveller Pedro Tafur saw carrier pigeons for the first time in 1436. The Republic of Genoa equipped their system of watch towers in the Mediterranean Sea with pigeon posts. *Tipu Sultan* of *Mysore* (1750-1799) also used messenger pigeons; they returned to the Jamia Masjid mosque in Srirangapatna, his headquarters: the pigeon holes can still be seen in the mosque's minarets.

By the 19th century homing pigeons were used extensively for military and other communications. During the *Franco-Prussian War* pigeons they carried mail between besieged Paris and the French unoccupied territory. In December 1870, it took ten hours for a pigeon carrying messages to fly from Perpignan to Brussels.

Historically, pigeons carried messages only one way, to their home. They had to be transported manually before another flight. However, by placing their food at one location and their home at another place, pigeons have been trained to fly back and forth up to twice a day, covering round-trip flights of up to 100 miles. Their reliability has lent itself to use on mail routes, such as the Great Barrier Pigeon-gram Service established between the *Auckland, New Zealand*, suburb of Newton and Great Barrier Island in November 1897, possibly the first regular air mail service in the world. The world's first 'airmail' stamps were issued for the Great Barrier *Pigeon-Gram Service* from 1898 to 1908.

A B–type bus from London converted into a pigeon loft for use in northern France and Belgium during the First World War

Dispatching a message by carrier pigeon within the Swiss Army during World War I

Crewman with the homing pigeons which were carried in bombers as a means of communication in the event of crashing, ditching, or radio failure

Homing pigeons were still employed in the 21st century by remote police departments in Odisha state in eastern India to provide emergency communication services following natural disasters but in March 2002, it was announced that India's Police Pigeon Service messenger system in Odisha was to be retired due to the expanded use of the Internet.

Most researchers believe that homing ability is based on a "map and compass" model, with the compass feature allowing birds to orient and the map feature allowing birds to determine their location relative to a goal site (home loft). The compass mechanism appears to rely on the sun, though the map mechanism has been highly debated.

Birds were used extensively during World War I. One homing pigeon, *Cher Ami*, was awarded the French Croix de guerre for her heroic service in delivering 12 important messages, despite having been very badly injured. During World War II, hundreds of homing pigeons with the Confidential Pigeon Service were airdropped into northwest Europe to serve as intelligence vectors for local resistance agents. Birds played a vital part in the Invasion of Normandy as radios could not be used for fear of vital information being intercepted by the enemy.

During the Second World War, the use of pigeons for sending messages was highlighted in Britain by the Princesses Elizabeth and Margaret as Girl Guides joining other Guides sending messages to the World Chief Guide in 1943, as part of a campaign to raise money for homing pigeons.

In September 2009, a South African IT company based in Durban pitted an eleven month old bird armed with a data packed 4 GB memory stick against the ADSL service from the country's biggest Internet service provider, Telkom. Remarkably, the pigeon, Winston, took an hour and eight minutes to carry all the data 50 miles while the data transfer took two hours, six minutes, and fifty-seven seconds.

Homing pigeons have also been used for smuggling, getting objects and narcotics secretly across borders and into prisons. For instance, between 2009 and 2015, pigeons have been reported to carry contraband items such as cell phones, SIM cards, phone *batteries* and USB cards into prisons in the Brazilian state of São Paulo. There have also been cases where homing pigeons were used to transport drugs into prisons.

The birds, as for migration, probably use a combination of learned landmarks with sensed direction (from the earth's magnetic field or from the sky) to identify where they are and so tonavigate. Internal "maps" are apparently constructed using vision, but other senses including olfaction and echolocation may also be used.

Al in all these long-distance navigational skills, still somewhat mysterious though possibly increasingly understood, show evidence of remarkable avian intelligence in a sphere for now outside normal human experience.

Communicators, songsters, and talkers

Birds, like humans, are social beings who communicate, and need to, each in our own ways – which, very different at first sight, may turn out when we look closer to be not so very different after all. When we consider the most recent research it seems that in this area there is much to learn and perhaps surprise.

Bird communicating

Birds communicate with their flock-mates and others through song, calls, and body language. There is a long background to all of this, and many studies.

The voice is the most noticeable form of bird communication. Bird use of sound includes singing, calls, squeaks, squawks, gurgles, warbles, trills, rattles, gulps, pops, whines, clicks, croaks, drums, whistles, howls, tremolos, honks and many other sorts of voiced noises.

We may not see them, but the air is full of sounds.

But it would be a mistake to assume that is *only* through vocalising that communication takes place. As with humans, it is a multi-sensory process. In fact, though vocalising is common, not *all birds* use their voices as their main method of communication. Some, like the ruffed grouse, make non-vocal sounds by beating the air with their wings to make a vacuum; the air rushes in to fill up that space and creates a kind of mini-sonic boom used to establish and hold a territory.

Another example: the Wilson's snipe, uses special tail feathers which it spreads during an earthward dive. As it plummets down, it beats its wings in a way that guides air through the feathers creating a winnowing sound. The snipe uses this during courtship.

Birds also communicate through visual displays. These are often a combination of behaviours and the feathers on the bird's body. In the case of blackbirds, the males puff up their feathers, lean forward, shrug their shoulders showing off their colourful shoulders, and exaggerate them with bold postures. They also sing out as they do this making their statement loud and clear.

We knew little as yet about the role of smell in avian communication though body odours may play some part on courting and mating, but touch certainly comes in. It is important in a negative sense in group flying – to avoid Interference and collision – but also more directly not only in physical fighting but also between nestlings, companions, mates, above all in the mutual kissing, cuddling, kissing, and grooming of devoted pairs alongside their side-by-side walking, swimming or flying.

It is in general the same among birds as among humans: a combination of senses are used to communicate.

That might seem to be it. But there is also the apparently non-sensory sense, as it were, that birds seem to share. Their as many-as-one flocking action is surely only possible through some form of communicating normally unknown to humans. So too with the way that one blue tit's new skill in getting at the cream spread near instantaneously throughout the country. How without some mysterious and to us humans unknown form of inter-communication did thousands of budgerigars gather in one spot in Australia on just one occasion?

There is clearly much still to discover about avian communication.

But let us continue with the aspects that we *do* know something about.

Why birds communicate?

Birds use their voices and bodies to communicate for many reasons: claiming territory, seeking mates, begging for food, calling their chicks or parent or mate, staying in touch with others, scolding an intruder of the same species or different species, announcing the presence of a predator, singing a duet with a mate and many other reasons. They use sound and action to scare off predators or warn other birds about danger, to attract a mate, or to defend their *territory*.

A budgerigar meet-up at Alice Springs: how did they arrange it?

Sound is a great form of communication because it can carry through obstacles and (especially good in forests) beyond where birds can see. In some cases, sounds can travel over a mile, even several miles under the right conditions. Also, if you are a bird that lives hidden in a thicket, your voice helps you stay in touch with your mate and with other members of your flock.

A green heron fledgling calls to its mother

Birds also tend to have very keen eyes so it is no surprise that visual displays are part of bird communication.

Look at the male red-winged blackbirds. They have deep black bodies, black wings, black heads and eyes, black tails and brilliant red and yellow wing patches. The red and yellow colours contrast starkly with the black, making these birds stunning to look at in full display. The way the males flash their brilliant wing patches as they sing enhances their messages. Both together are used by the birds to convey that they are claiming this patch.

Such displays don't go unnoticed by the females. Females of most bird species are generally duller looking in colour compared to the males and are very critical of the appearance of males. When choosing a mate they don't just listen to his song, but also closely scrutinise his appearance and actions.

Why, you might ask? No doubt the healthier and more impressive a male birds feathers are, the healthier are his genes. Females want to mate with only the best males. If he sings well and has great plumage, she will want him to father her chicks. Or perhaps the display is just appealing in itself?

Though a different species we can learn to understand something of bird communication. For example, the beautiful visual displays of a peacock or red-winged blackbird, or the enchanting song of a wood thrush can touch us all on a personal level even if. that experience and the meaning we gain from it is different for each of us.

Nothing birds do is without a purpose. There are many levels of meaning in bird communication. On one level there are the colours and patterns on a bird, a signal that "I belong to this species". Each species of bird looks and sounds different, distinguishing whether a bird is a possible mate or not.

On another level, a bird's physical behaviour communicates: for example, if it is feeding calmly, flying away, hiding from a potential threat. Since birds can puff out or flatten down their feathers at will, how the feathers look helps to convey how the bird is feeling and what it is wanting to communicate.

Bird communication changes with times of the year in any given location, so in many parts of the world, birds are strongly affected by the four seasons. Winter, for instance, is often the quieter time for vocalising with singing getting going again in the spring.

Song

Songbirds make up almost half of the world's 10,000 bird species, among them warblers, thrushes, and sparrows. Yellow warblers for example are classic songbirds

Beautiful to hear, but for the singer there are costs. Singing is both expensive in energy and liable to alert predators.

So then why do birds sing? Evidence suggests that it is both to proclaim and defend their territories and – a crucial role – help in attracting and impressing potential mates by signifying the overall health and ability of the singer. As with humans, singing is a chance to show off. Birdsong is in fact more like music than a language. Birds sing to attract mates and defend territories, and the information in a song is basically just "Listen to my song, isn't it beautiful?" or "Keep out, this place belongs to me!"

It is mostly males who sing. The majority of female songbirds in temperate zones use shorter, simpler calls while the males produce longer and more complex vocalising. In the tropics however females commonly sing, and many species engage in duetting.

Northern cardinals can switch sides of their syrinx

In songbirds, each side of the syrinx is independently controlled, allowing birds, unlike humans, to produce two unrelated pitches at once. Some birds even have the ability to sing rising and falling notes simultaneously, like the wood thrush in its final trill. This makes vocal gymnastics possible. For example, the northern cardinal can sweep through more notes than are on a piano keyboard in just a tenth of a second. Because each branch of the songbird syrinx is individually controlled, cardinal birds can start its notes with one side of the syrinx and seamlessly switch to the other side without stopping for a breath (the envy of human vocalists!).

Birds often sing more intensely at dawn than at any other time of the day. This singing may well be warnings given by male birds in defence of their territory and mate but we don't really know why birds concentrate their efforts in the dawn chorus. Maybe it's partly just joy to welcome the day.

How do birds know how to sing? and what?

It seems that some birds hatch already knowing the songs they will sing as adults. But the true songbirds have to *learn* how to sing. They begin when they are still in the nest by listening to the adults singing, like a young thrush listening to a parent's song which it will later try to copy.

Eastern meadowlarks mark territory with song

Learning to sing (Barber 1994, photo Jack Dermid)

After fledging, they try to replicate these songs, practising until they have matched them. The intricate territorial songs of some birds have to be learned at an early age, and as well as, for some birds, the sometimes huge repertoire of their own newly-composed sings, the memory of that first-heard song will serve the bird for the rest of its life.

Some songbirds, such as the catbirds, thrashers, and mockingbirds, learn to mimic other species – frogs, cats, and even car alarms. Lyrebirds, large songbirds living in forests in Australia are famous for their incredible ability to realistically mimic sounds – from forest creatures to chainsaws and drills – as well as putting on elaborate song and dance displays for potential female mates.

Some bird species are able to communicate in a number of regional varieties of their songs. For example, the New Zealand saddlebacks learn the different song "dialects" of their own species clans, much as human beings acquire diverse regional dialects. This often happens when populations of the same species are isolated by geographic features such as mountains, bodies of water, or stretches of unsuitable habitat. These local dialects are then passed on to the next generation of young birds, which hear the songs being performed by their father and other local males. After many generations, the birds from one area can get to sound quite different from those on the next mountain.

When a territory-owning male of the species dies, a young male will immediately take his place, singing to prospective mates in the dialect appropriate to the territory he is in. Similarly, around 300 tui songs have been recorded. The greater the competition in the area, the more likely the birds are to make their songs extra complex (more on the creativity and music of birdsong in the next chapter).

Inter-species communicating – humans and birds

It is one of the extraordinary facts of nature that different species can in some ways communicate with each other. We know this. Anyone who has ridden a horse with understanding, or loved a pet, or engaged in hands-on sheep or cattle farming knows this. So, remarkably indeed, birds and humans *can* communicate: dinosaurs with mammals.

Only up to a point, it is true, and certainly not always in verbal language. But it happens.

Birds certainly understand certain kinds of human speech. I well remember calling out to our hens: "Chucky Chucky Chucky Chucky Chucky" (quick high notes) and they knew exactly that I was telling them their food was ready; or "Ducks ducks here y'are" for the ducks in the pond to know we were about to thrown them pieces of bread so come quick; budgie owners have developed shared, mainly vocal, ways to be understood by their caged pets; companion ravens have long engaged in active communication with their owners – and much else.

And then there was the way, as we saw earlier, that the honey birds came and listened to the Yao speakers' *"brr hm"*, understanding they were being told that their joint quest for honeycombs was about to start. There are also records of more sophisticated and consistent cases of human speaking with birds with remarkable understanding (more on this in the description of Alex a little later).

In each case one party takes the lead in talking, it is true, but in neither case is he or she alone, for the one must teach or provide an example, the other must copy or respond. Talk is interactive not just one way.

And then there are the ways birds are understood to communicate with humans

This goes back to the ancient world and no doubt, if we had but the evidence, beyond. Throughout earlier history, parrots, canaries, and other talking birds have been kept as beloved pets – often a status symbol too – and depicted lovingly in art and literature.

In the Indian Rig-Veda, written more than 3,000 years ago, talking parrots were considered to be birds of love and the subject of fables, early Chinese poetry speaks of talking birds, and the ancient Egyptians kept African grey parrots as pets. The Romans were fascinated by talking parrots: those from India being especially popular among the elite in Rome where professional black parrot-teachers were employed to teach the birds to speak Latin.

In more recent times talking birds are mentioned in Chaucer's *Canterbury Tales,* while Pope Martin V in Rome had a "Keeper of the Parrots" to ensure his talking birds received the highest level of care. One of the greatest lovers of talking birds was Henry VIII of England, who kept his beloved African grey parrot at Hampton Court in the sixteenth century. France had a cage-makers guild dedicated to fashioning fine bird homes for the upper class, and Louis XV and Louis XVI both commissioned elaborate cages and aviaries for the Versailles gardens.

Today, parrots and other talking birds are more popular than ever. Bird clubs exist for pet owners, with a focus on owner education and optimal bird care, and thousands of families own budgerigars or other communicative birds.

Is it "language"?

Are we to call this interactive bird communicating "language", either in the wild or in trained talking with humans? In either of these contexts is it just automatic responses or blind mimicking with no cognitive *understanding*? And is it informed by *conceptual* understanding and the power to generalise from single isolated instances? Is it really deliberate "language" at all?

Ethnologists, linguists and comparative psychologists now pay attention to the complex communicative abilities of animals, including the possible syntactic ability of songbirds. The detailed observational and experimental data recently gathered in this area has increased the general interest in comparative communication systems and the possible parallels between humans, birds' and nonhuman primates. As a result, avian verbal / vocal combinations are now a topic of intense debate and speculation, involving a great deal of observational and experimental research, both systematic and (not to be scorned) anecdotal / case study based.

It largely depends of course on how you define "language". Given the many contending approaches and interpretations to both this and the evidence, it is no surprise that most conclusions remain for now controversial.

But at least the term *bird language* would certainly seem appropriate in a general sense for referring to bird vocalisations that successfully communicate information to other birds or other animals in general. In this sense bird calls do indeed make up a language in which birds convey meanings that are interpreted correctly by their listeners. Domestic *chickens*, for example, like other birds, have distinctive alarm calls for aerial and ground predators, and they respond to these alarm calls appropriately and with understanding.

Some have argued that in order for a communication system to count as a *language* it must go behind isolated words / sounds / calls to link these together and be able to apply the combinations in appropriate situations: to be *"combinatorial"* or "compositional" in having an open-ended set of grammar-compliant elements made from a finite vocabulary. This would be a syntax in the sense of a set of rules for combining words into phrases in which the meaning of a combination depends on both the meaning of its parts and the way in which they are combined.

It can thus be argued that to demonstrate compositional syntax in non-human animals three conditions need to apply: (i) call sequences depending on the context; (ii) response to the sequence with an understanding of the meanings of the separate components, plus (iii) responding to the whole, combined, sequence. A recent study (https://tinyurl.com/2p8n7rk3) based on prolonged observation and experiment, shows that the Japanese tits' call system meets these conditions. They have over ten different notes in their vocal repertoire and use them either singly or in combination with other notes. They produce what we could call "ABC" calls (warning of predators), and "D" calls ("come here", attracting attention from other members of their species). Interestingly, they combine these two into "ABC-D" sequences when recruiting their fellows to mob a predator. They behave differently when hearing ABC calls (moving their heads horizontally as if scanning for danger) and D calls (a call to come near). In response to ABC-D sequences, they do both of these things.

It seems further that tits *combine* different meaningful signals to generate a compound message that depends on the meaning of the elements and the way in which they are combined, i.e., compositional syntax. So the tits are using language like humans, joining specific "chirrups" together – combining their tweets – to form complex sentences and communicate new messages, arguably the first non-human creature shown to do so. Their system may have nothing approaching the range and coverage of human language but it perfectly meets the tits' wants and needs. Black capped chickadees' *innate* vocalisations have also been intensively studied and recorded in the wild, and shown to have a similar kind if combinatorial structure.

Narrow definitions of language would insist that, in addition to isolated/sounds/calls, however well understood, a language in the strict sense has to have *grammar*. Research on, for example, parrots suggests an innate ability for grammatical structures, including the existence of concepts such as nouns, adjectives and verbs. Studies of parakeets have shown a striking similarity between talking bird's verbal areas in the brain and the equivalent human brain areas, suggesting that in humans too – think of a child gradually learning to speak – mimicry has much to do with the construction of language and its structures and order.

Many analysts, including myself, would elaborate this by positing that language must have some *conceptual* underpinning – the ability, which certainly we humans have, to *generalise* from otherwise isolated instances and apply these concepts appropriately to new instances.

Evidence that birds can do this and form abstract concepts in their calls such as "same vs. different" has been provided by some parrots and corvids, in particular by a famous grey parrot named Alex, to be described shortly.

Previously it had been thought it was only humans and great apes and perhaps elephants that we could see from another individual's point of view and, apparently, attribute motivations and desires to them. But a study of the little green bee-eater suggests that these birds are able to see from another's viewpoint, in this case that of a potential predator, and thus react to its likely behaviour. Similarly, California scrub jays who hide caches of food will re–hide it if they have been watched by another bird, but only if it knows that that one had stolen food before. Again, a male Eurasian jay takes into account which food his mate prefers when feeding her during courtship feeding rituals.

A remarkable case of avian vocal learning and accomplishment is that of the talking African grey parrot called Alex, "the talking bird".

Alex was trained by animal psychologist Irene Pepperberg to vocally label more than 100 objects of different colours and shapes and detect and name the material from each was made. Alex also could, and did, request or refuse these objects ("I want X" etc) according to his wishes on the day. He also – and this is surely a real sign of intelligent understanding – acted as a "teacher" for younger grey parrots in the lab. Alex would often observe and listen to the teaching, verbally correcting the younger parrot or calling out a correct answer before the learner could give a response.

To quote from Dr. Pepperberg's account, Alex was "able to participate in some forms of inter-species communication", demonstrating more than simply the ability to mimic human speech patterns. He was taught to vocally identify certain objects, like "key" and *paper*, by name, also to name certain colours such as "green" and "blue", and certain shapes with labels like "three corner" in order to categorise objects with respect to colour and shape. He also learned to recognise quantities of objects up to five and the functional use of the word "no" as well as phrases such as "come here" and "wanna go".

When an object was held up before him, he identified it accurately eight times out of ten. His most frequent errors were either the omission of the colour or shape adjectives, or the unclear pronunciation of the colour adjectives. For example, when the trainer held up a green key and said "What's this?" Alex answered "green key" only 69% of the times. If the answer that he gave was simply "key" as it often was, the researcher then put the question "What colour key?". Alex usually got it right second try, raising the score from 69% to 94%. When randomly shown unfamiliar objects of familiar colours, the bird could not, of course, identify the objects, but invariably got the colour right.

Whenever he incorrectly identified an object, Alex was told "no". After about 18 months of training, he began to use the word to his trainer when he appeared to wish not to be handled. Trainers then started to use the word "No" when refusing to relinquish an item Alex wanted. Soon after this, when refusing to identify a proffered object, Alex would say "No". He also used "No" to reject unacceptably small pieces of food, and toys he no longer liked. In many cases he made his refusals extra clear by turning his head away.

To my mind what was most striking was the way Alex was able to understand and extend the use of the word "No" from an assertion by his trainer that Alex had got the answer wrong to his own wishes and intentions – definitely a recognition of the *concept* of "No", extending it from a specific case to a general concept.

Besides using words whose use he had been taught, Alex spontaneously but meaningfully used other words he had just picked up. For example, although he had not been taught to use labels for foods, he requested food items or objects by speaking their names, prefaced by "want".

If a trainer took a favourite object, say a cork, out of a drawer and Alex saw it, he would say "want cork". He also asked for objects not in view. And if a wrong object was offered, he either said "No" and refused to take it, or threw it back!

There was also Alex's remarkable creative ability in using new combinations of words. For example, having previously been taught to identify certain objects as "green" and a clothes peg as the object "peg wood" (but never as a green one) the bird was offered a green clothes peg. He said "green wood, peg wood". Later on first-ever presentation he identified "blue peg wood", "green cork" and "blue hide". To segment phrases and recombine the elements in this way is to begin to meet one crucial criterion in the definition of true language.

Cognitive studies

Leaving aside language, what about bird intelligence in general? This too is an elusive and highly controversial subject – for humans also of course.

There are many *studies*, but – as, again, for human intelligence – it is a problematic subject that depends on definitions as much as on field or laboratory findings. Some of the avian findings however are by any standards astonishing.

In general, birds have relatively large brains compared to their head size. The visual and auditory senses are well developed in most species, though the tactile and olfactory senses are well realised only in a few groups. As we have seen birds communicate using visual signals as well as through calls and song. The testing of intelligence in birds is therefore usually based on studying responses to these sensory stimuli.

This fits with recent approaches in cognitive studies. For humans, "intelligence" is often (though not invariably) approached from what people *do*, and appear from their actions *do with deliberate understanding and intention*, rather than speculating about the inner unseen doings of the brain waves

The same with birds.

There have now been many *studies* of birds such as quail, domestic fowl, pigeons. finches, and birds of prey. Most have perforce been of birds kept under captive conditions and (unlike for apes) field studies in natural conditions have been limited. Nevertheless, the results have been illuminating.

From research with captive birds, the most closely studied and revealing cases have been those corvids (ravens, crows, jays, magpies, etc.) and *psittacines* (parrots, macaws, and cockatoos). As a result, these are now generally considered the most intelligent birds, and among the most intelligent animals in general.

In 2014, for example, a New Caledonian crow named "007" by researchers in New Zealand solved an eight-step puzzle to get to some food.

Keas are also known for their intelligence and curiosity, both vital traits for survival in the harsh mountain environment where they live. They can solve logical puzzles, such as pushing and pulling things in a certain order to get to food, and will work together – social beings again – to achieve a jointly desired objective.

Counting has traditionally been considered another ability that shows intelligence. Some studies have suggested that crows may indeed have a true numerical ability: that parrots can count up to 6 and crows up to 8. Cormorants too: used by Chinese fishermen to catch fish they were given every eighth fish as a reward. Once their quota of seven fish was completed, the birds refused to move again while those who had not yet filled their quotas continued to catch as usual. Many birds are also able to detect changes in the number of eggs in their nest, and brood and parasitic cuckoos are known to remove one of the host eggs before laying their own.

The ability of animals to *learn* by observation and imitation is considered more significant than reward-induced responses. Crows – highly social creatures – are noted for their ability to learn from each other, and of course their observational and deliberate manipulative skills, as in the dismantling of the child' tricycle described earlier, are by now well-known – another mark, it would generally be agreed, of one form of applied intelligence.

The apt use of observation and learning can also be taken as a sign of intelligence, something certainly to be found among birds. To the examples of planning and foresight built on experience described in an earlier chapter, we could add the remarkable case of the starlings who, among certain other birds, deliberately seek out the green leaves of certain aromatic plants and place them in their nests specifically, it appears, to keep parasites such as lice at bay – which they do.

Pigeons too have featured in numerous experiments in comparative psychology, so there is now considerable knowledge of their intelligence. For example:

- Pigeons can be taught complex actions and response sequences, and can learn to make responses in different sequences.
- Pigeons readily learn to respond in the presence of one simple stimulus and withhold responding in the presence of a different stimulus, or to make different responses in the presence of different stimuli.
- Pigeons can discriminate between other individual pigeons, and can use the behaviour of another individual as a cue to tell them what response to make.
- Pigeons readily learn to make discriminative responses to different categories of stimuli, defined either by arbitrary rules (e.g. green triangles) or by human concepts (e.g. pictures of human beings).

- Pigeons can remember large numbers of individual images for a long time, e.g. hundreds of images for periods of several years.
- In addition, pigeons have unusual, perhaps unique, abilities to learn routes back to their home from long distances. This homing behaviour is different from that of birds that learn migration routes, which usually occurs over a fixed route at fixed times of the year, whereas homing is more flexible; however similar mechanisms may be involved.

An interesting demonstration of their unusual intelligence is that rock dove pigeons, who share many visual properties with humans and are promising surrogate observers of medical images, are able to distinguish benign from malignant human breast histopathology images and apply this learning to previously unseen images – an amazing and most unusual capability.

Remarkably, pigeons can also be taught to discriminate between paintings by Picasso and by Monet. The birds were first trained on a limited set of paintings: when the shown painting was a Picasso, the pigeon was able to obtain food by repeated pecking; when it was a Monet, pecking had no effect. After a while, the pigeons would only peck when shown Picasso paintings. They were by then able to generalise so as to correctly distinguish paintings by the two that they had not previously seen, and even between cubist and *impressionist* paintings, When the Monet paintings were shown upside down, the pigeons were not able to categorise them, while – how intelligent! – upside down *cubist* works did not have same effect. They also learned to distinguish p photos showing human beings from those that did not, and between photos showing trees and those that didn't (and many similar examples).

In all these cases, intelligent discrimination is relatively easy for humans, even though the classes are so complex that no simple distinguishing algorithm or rule can be specified. It has therefore been hypothesised P – though controversially – that pigeons can form "concepts" or "categories" similar to humans. Why not?

Birds belonging to the by now well-studied crow and parrot families, finally, are interesting not just as individuals, though some of these are remarkable, but in a more general way by bearing on the question of what factors are generally important as necessary or sufficient conditions for intelligence. Like humans, they are known to live socially, have lengthy developmental periods and long lives (fit span for learning and sharing the results of that learning), and are attuned to travelling widely, thus necessarily taking on new ways as they adapt to different environments. Also, important and running through all this, they are capable of *learning,* surely a key foundation and condition for intelligence (in whatever sense we wish to understand that elusive term),

In addition, though it is not easy to assess the significance of this, birds ppossess large forebrains and high vocal centres, which have been hypothesised to be related to greater cognitive ability. Harvey J. Karten, a neuroscientist who has studied the physiology of birds, has noted that the lower parts of avian brains are similar to those of humans, presumably a case of convergent evolution.

Recognition of identity?

Finally, do birds, presumably like humans, recognise individuality in others and themselves? It seems from observation and multiple experiments that some birds at least can and do.

Christine Stracey for example remembers the first time a mockingbird dive-bombed her head. She had been visiting nests in her neighbourhood, counting eggs and banding chicks for a research project. Over time, she noticed that the birds were getting aggressive, squawking and swooping at her as soon as they saw her coming. The mockingbirds focused on Stracey, ignoring passersby, even gardeners working right underneath their nests. "By the end of the summer, I was absolutely convinced that the birds knew me and did not like me!" she says.

The idea that birds can recognise individual humans isn't new. Any parrot owner will tell you that their pet knows the difference between its owner and a stranger and scientists have shown that crows can identify people by sight. In one experiment, the birds scolded researchers in the caveman masks they had worn when catching and banding them months earlier, but ignored "neutral" figures wearing Dick Cheney masks.

Since there seemed to be no published work on *wild* birds' ability to recognise people and mockingbirds aren't considered to be as intelligent as parrots or crows, Stracey designed an experiment to see if mockingbirds could really recognise individuals. First, she and her colleagues located a brooding mockingbird on campus, then got one volunteer to stand near the nest for 30 seconds and touch it for half of that time on four consecutive days while the mother mockingbird was present. With each visit, the bird grew more agitated. At first, the mother bird waited until the person came close and then flew to a nearby bush to shout out alarm calls, a behaviour called "flushing" that birds do to distract predators in the wild. By the fourth day, she or her mate was already up and dive-bombed the volunteer's head.

On the fifth day, the team got a completely new person to approach the nest: the mother bird reset her behaviour, responding as she had to the other volunteer on the first day. The mockingbirds were able to spot their intruder out of the hundreds of people who passed their nest each day,

Here is one way it worked out. There is a park in Paris where pigeons love to gather. Two researchers of similar build, hair and skin tone met, armed with bird food, but wearing different coloured lab coats. Both gave food to the pigeons who happily devoured it.

The first researcher, A, sat back and left them to it. The second shooed the birds away when the food was finished.

They waited a while and fed them again. This time, neither researcher shooed the birds away, however, the pigeons gravitated toward the "nice guy", A. This happened consistently at multiple attempts. Then they swapped their lab coats. The clever pigeons still went to researcher A, clearly not fooled by the outfit change, instead they recognised facial features or, perhaps, what we could call someone's essential identity.

Crows are especially renowned for having long memories and holding grudges, as you will know if one has ever dive-bombed you. It can lead to years of revenge, not just from him, but also from his "gang". Upset a crow and he will memorise your face, and scold you from a distance, screeching noise being both a warning to you and a battle-cry to other birds from his community. All will commit your face to memory and you could face retribution from any one of the gang for up to five years! All in all, crows remember faces, including not only those they dislike but anyone who has observed them catching food.

Skuas too (Antarctic seabirds) are clever enough to recognise individual humans after seeing them only a few times. In the winter of 2014-2015, some researchers visited skua nests once a week to check on their eggs and chicks. They suspected that the birds were unhappy about humans poking at their nests (if a skua wants you to go away, it will give not-so-subtle hints like attacking your head) and would recognise them again – and so it proved.

There is also recognition of individuals *within* the species. Birds recognise each other by their voices or calls. They can identify mates, parents or offspring by voice, much as a blind person might do. During courtship and pair formation, birds probably learn to recognise their mate by "voice" characteristics more than by visual appearance.

Konrad Lorenz built on this in his demonstration that jackdaws have "names" that identify each individual in the flock. During flight preparations each of them say one other bird's name, thus creating a chain. It is cross-species too. In his book *King Solomon's Ring,* he describes the name he was given by the birds and how, amazingly, he was recognised years later in a far-away location.

And "self-aware", whatever that means (an elusive question for humans too)? But when we think about it, can we really believe that the proud courting swan is unaware of his proud male selfhood, or indeed the shy female of her situation and herself being wooed? or parents unaware of their love and pride when looking at their offsprings' first attempts to fly? or perhaps the raven carefully working out the best way to solve the dilemma of reaching his food and formulate a plan? or all those other show-off males?

Are not humans too fully aware of selfhood and individual identity without necessarily having to formulate this in *verbal* terms. Do we have to think of birds, those intelligent and deliberate communicators, as being so very different?

The art of birds

The lives of birds and humans have long been entwined so it is no surprise that birds feature prominently, and everywhere, in human art.

Birds fascinate us. They are everywhere that we have settled on earth, and in many places we have not. We admire them for their shapes, feathers, and song, and are inspired by their beauty and their music. We are also sometimes, too, annoyed or scared by them. So, it is little wonder that birds have inspired so much art, music, and folklore, from the dove that was the harbinger of the end of the great flood to the swallows that signal the start of summer.

Art, play and display

First however a word about birds themselves – do *they* have an aesthetic sense? Can we find any avian parallels to *homo ludens*, a being of play and art?

The answer would seem to be yes. It is not only humans, it appears, who have a feeling for beauty – or indeed, as we have seen, for play, for love, and for sorrow, the roots of art and of tragedy.

With no apparent practical benefit golden eagles adorn their stark nests with sprigs of green boughs throughout the nesting season and after, and magpies, black kites and bald eagles are famous for gathering up beautiful things. They seek out baubles and trinkets to decorate their nests – a feeling, perhaps, less for thievery, the popular image, than for artistic collection.

Bower bird gathering treasures for his bower

Then there are the amazing structures built by male bowerbirds – not functional nests, more show-stages and dance floors. They are built to display to females, who, it seems, are attracted to larger more ornate structures and judge a male on his collection of treasures.

The *functional* nest is built by the female after she has been mated by her chosen male. She incubates the eggs and raises the young on her own, while the male stays with his bower to attract more females.

Simple bowers consist of an avenue of twigs in which a male bird walks up and down to display himself to females. In some the sticks have been painted with yellow, brown or purple plant juices. More complicated bowers are towers of sticks and display arenas on which the male arranges his collection and around which he displays himself. Treasures include feathers, particularly blue ones, snail shells, beetle wings, bones, flowers, and anything else which takes the bird's fancy. They may include man-made objects such as silver spoons, car keys, gun cartridges, tin mugs, buttons, and colourful scraps of material.

The most impressive bowers are built by vogelkop gardener birds from New Guinea. It can be a huge open-fronted roofed hut over two yards tall and two or more yards across – built by a bird no bigger a song thrush! In front of it he dances and shows himself off (look at shorturl.at/ mzWY1) while the courted female watches.

And then, as with presents of flowers to human loves, male birds in some species bring selections of beautiful flowers to their mates. Fairy wren males find and pick petals in colours contrasting with their bright nuptial plumage and present them to others of their species who acknowledge, inspect, and sometimes manipulate the petals. This is seems, not to be linked to sexual or aggressive activity; it's apparently just because they see the flowers as attractive – or, you might say, just for the sake of beauty.

And then there is avian music. As we have seen, this also has utilitarian functions – as of course does, in part, all music. But birds *also* seem just to sing for its own sake – "listen to my pretty sing, *I* love it too". Who is to say that they have less appreciation of the beauty of music than do humans, or less satisfaction than us in showing off their art?

And again, as for humans, life is not all serious or utilitarian. There is also room for *fun* … for, that is, activities with no obvious immediate benefits. Cockatoos have been filmed in marvellous dancing in perfect rhythm (look up the "Cockatoo dances to Elvis original" video, you'll be amazed), a parrot joining in the dance at a party, the incredible show–off aerobatics of courting males. Some birds, notably crows, parrots and birds of prey, famously play with objects just for fun. They enjoy themselves in flight letting stones, sticks or leaves go, then catching them again before they reach the ground so as to repeat the game. Some pick up objects to play with, or repeatedly drop stones, apparently to enjoy the sound effects. Similarly, some ducks float through tidal rapids or fast-moving sections of rivers, then hurry back to the top to ride down over and over, while ravens and crows rise on air currents only to swoop down, then glide back upwards, again and again. Young blue jays, belonging to what is accepted to be a highly intelligent and notably curious species, playfully snatch brightly coloured or reflective objects, such as bottle caps or pieces of aluminium foil, and carry them around until they lose interest.

Ravens sometimes make their own toys, for example breaking off twigs to play with. A film captured a bird and puppy playing delightedly together, another of a corvid and dog playing with a table tennis ball (shorturl.at/atDY3 and shorturl.at/szNX6), yet another showed a crow sliding down a snow-covered roof balanced precariously with flapping

wings on a tray then struggling back up to start again. Young crows sometimes enjoy a tug-of-war game, and crows and ravens have been filmed playing in the snow, rolling in it, striding joyously across it, making snowballs – what can all this be but for fun?

While play might also serve to increase survival skills, some birds do seem, like humans, to play just for the sheer joy and fun of the activity. Why not?

Birds and music

Birds are not only, it seems, the *inspiration and model* for human music, they also feature *in* it – another of the many uses of birds for human life and art.

Birds have played a role in western classical music since at least the 14th century, when composers such as Jean Vaillant quoted birdsong in their compositions. Among the birds whose song is most often used in music are the nightingale and the cuckoo.

The nightingale's song has been particularly prominent. Handel used it in the aria "Sweet bird" in *L'Allegro, il Penseroso ed il Moderato*, in the "Nightingale chorus" in *Solomon*, and in the Organ Concerto known as "The Cuckoo and the Nightingale". It comes in Rameau's opera *Hippolyte, Respighi*'s *The Birds,* and Beethoven's *Pastoral Symphony*. Nightingales come in music by *Glinka*, Mendelssohn, Liszt, Balakirev, Grieg, Granados, Ravel, and *Milhaud.*

The cuckoo's distinctive call is heard clearly in, among others, Beethoven (*Pastoral Symphony*), Delius (*On Hearing the First Cuckoo in Spring*), Handel *(The Cuckoo and the Nightingale)*, Respighi (*The Birds*), Rimsky-Korsakov (*Snow Maidens*), Saint-Saens (*Carnival of the Animals*), and Vivaldi (*Concerto in A*). An early example of a composition that imitates birdsong is the cuckoo in *Janequin*'s 16th century *Le Chant Des Oiseaux.*

Though less commonly imitated, we also hear songs of the great tit (Bruckner), *goldfinch* (Vivaldi), linnet (Couperin, Haydn and *Rachmaninov*), robin (Peter Warlock), swallow (Dvorak and Tchaikovsky), wagtail (Benjamin Britten), and magpie (Mussorgsky). Dvorak celebrated many kinds of bird, including doves, skylarks, and house sparrows.

Nightingales are admired for their unusually rich song

Composers and musicians make use of birds' music in a variety of ways: they can be inspired by birdsong; they can intentionally imitate bird song; they can incorporate recordings of birds into their works, as *Ottorino Respighi* did; or, like the cellist Beatrice Harrison in 1924 and more recently the *jazz musician* David Rothenberg, they can duet with birds.

Pied butcherbird vocalisations have been the source of compositional design in melody, harmony, rhythm, gesture, contour, dynamic envelope, formal structure, phrase length, the balance of sound and silence, scales, repetition, acoustic image, programmatic intent, and poetic or psychic inspiration. Their flute-like phrases have been assigned to piano and bass, clarinet and bassoon, xylophone and violin.

Among *jazz musicians*, Paul Winter (*Flyway*) and Jeff Silverbush (*Grandma Mickey*) made use of birdsong-like sounds. The *improvisatory* saxophonist Charlie Parker, known as "Bird", played fast, flowing melodic lines, with titles such as *Yardbird Suite, Ornithology, Bird Gets the Worm, and Bird of Paradise.*

Imani Sanga identifies three ways that bird song is classified and perceived in an African context: that birds sing, are musicians, and are materials for composition. He notes that Western musicians likewise use birds in compositions and cites Steven Feld's observation that in *Kaluli* music in Papua New Guinea, birds are perceived as spirits that want to communicate with the living through their singing. San describes stories he grew up with in Africa, commenting that people make stories about birds to explain their presence around them. His perception of birds like ringed-neck doves and hornbills, he says, influences his life every day.

Composers have a variety of bird sounds to work with, from actual birdsong and calls to the appearance and movements of birds, whether real, fictional (like the phoenix) or even mechanical.

They can choose to use these materials literally, imitating the sounds, as when Sergei Prokofiev uses an oboe for the quacking of a duck in *Peter and the Wolf*; to represent the birds symbolically; or to give a general impression, as when Vivaldi paints a picture of birds moving and singing in *The Four Seasons*. Sibelius claimed that the crane's call was the "leitmotiv of my life", imitated by clarinets in "Scene with Cranes" in his incidental music from Kuolema, and Vaughan Williams' *The Lark Ascending* opens with a silvery solo violin, then flutters and darts, reaching up higher and higher above the orchestra's hushed, held chord. Hanna Tuulikki's *Away with the Birds* (2013) is composed of traditional Gaelic songs and poems which imitate birdsong; its five movements represent waders, seabirds, wildfowl, corvids, and the cuckoo.

The Italian composer Ottorino Respighi in *The Pines of Rome* (1923/4) was possibly the first to compose a piece of music that includes actual, pre–recorded, birdsong. A few years later, he wrote *Gli Uccelli (The Birds),* based on baroque pieces imitating four different birds, one to each movement of the work after its prelude, while the Finnish composer Einojuhani Rautavaara's *Concerto for Birds and Orchestra* has recorded birdsong and bird calls such as the trumpeting of migrating swans.

In the 1960s and 1970s, rock bands such as Pink Floyd started to use sound effects including birdsong in their albums the English singer Kate Bush used bird calls on her 2005 album, *Aerial*.

Rothenberg among several other writers has claimed that some birds such as the hermit thrush sing on the traditional scales used in human music. Among birds like starlings their variations of rhythm, relationships of musical pitch, and combinations of notes also resemble human music, and bird music can have human-like song structures such as arch-shaped and descending melodic contours, long notes at the ends of musical phrases, and typically small differences in pitch between adjacent notes.

The consonance between avian and human music was brought out further in a 1924 BBC radio programme in which Beatrice Harrison played the cello in her garden alongside singing nightingales attracted by her playing. The philosopher and jazz musician David Rothenberg similarly played an impromptu duet in March 2000 with a laughingthrush at the National Aviary in Pittsburgh. In the wild, male and female thrushes sing complex duets, and, following their natural behaviour, "jammed" with a human clarinet player. Rothenberg has also recorded a duet with an Australian lyrebird. In *Why Birds Sing*, Rothenberg claims that birds vocalise traditional scales used in human music. He argues that birds like the hermit thrush sing on the *pentatonic scale*, while the wood thrush sings on the *diatonic scale*, evidence that birdsong not only sounds like music, but *is* music in a human sense.

In the light of these and similar examples many musicologists now believe that birdsong not only generally underlies but has gone a long way to shape many aspects of human music, indeed is, perhaps, its ultimate origin.

Birds in art

The beauty, colour and flight of birds have attracted artists from prehistoric times to the present, and in multiple formats. Pictures speak louder than words, so here we go. Sometimes it's just in decorative bits and pieces, household, street, personal adornment.

Birds are a favourite subject in decorative displays all round home from cushions and curtains, table-ware, wallpaper, to drying cloths, scarfs and dress materials – even the cover of my ironing board in my kitchen.

They come magnificently on coins and postage stamps from all over the world. Tuvalu, a small Pacific island, made created a new income, its main resource, from the wonderful birds their stamps displayed in its postage stamps, the same for several other countries.

Birds come on weather vanes, in friezes, in statues, in pictographic writing from the earliest times …

When in doubt over a greeting card, a bird is pretty well always a safe choice.

Sometimes birds appear just in decorative bits and pieces, household, street, or public building, past and present, jewellery, and weather vanes,

Pictures and Christmas cards (*homo socialis* again), where robins *are* as popular as *Santa Claus, doves too, for peace.* Birds are used as humorous take-offs of human idiosyncrasies, or as high minded and beautiful symbols of the natural world.

Book covers, picture books, illustrations.

Emblems and symbolic displays of every kind, in every context from colourful popular art… to the highest of high art.

Merry Christmas

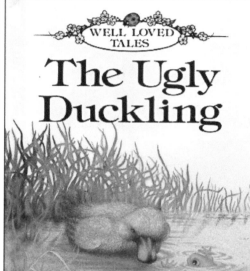

Happy Birthday

Birds in mythology

Bird symbols are prominent in many religions, many times, many cultures, especially in the Middle East, Asia and Native America. The meanings vary but they often represent immortality, departed souls, and spirit messengers, representing fertility, protection, and strength. In *feng shui* philosophy for example birds are compelling symbols because they can fly with freedom from the earth; they soar through the sky, connecting us to the heavens, the living embodiment of what many religious scripts and leaders tell, as symbols of hope and strength.

Ninth-century Irish manuscript, Christ enthroned between two birds

Birds appear again and again in crucial events in the Bible as symbols of mercy, hope, and divine intervention. It is a bird that carries the Israelites to safety on her wings and a bird that brings back the olive branch to Noah signifying the end of the legendary flood. A bird accompanies Jesus on his first temple visit, birds bring bread to the prophets when they are hungry, hope when they feel defeated or alone, and relief when they feel anxious. Birds can be the best form of medication for those in spiritual pain or heartbreak.

Birds come in dreams and in augury too, with various, but always profoundly personal, meaning. They often seem to mean harmony, balance, joy, ecstasy, and love, but can also deliver warnings and foreshadow terrible times, struggles, or difficulties.

Here are what have come to be some recurrent representations and meanings:

Cranes – *Peace, blessings, good luck*
Eagles – Courage, rebirth, power
Owls – *Insight, wisdom, death*
Swans – Light, twin flame, purity
Sparrows – *Productivity, diligence, creativity*
Peacocks – Serenity, spring, vanity
Nightingales – *Anticipation, love, secrets*
Crows – Transformation, change, adaption.

They take varied forms however depending on the specific culture. Many Native American clan members for example recall enchanting tales, legends, and stories about different species of birds, with almost all tales ending with a moral to teach the value of life to their young members. Ancient Celts on the other hand regarded birds as reincarnations of the most pious and highly respected individuals, standing for transcendence, freedom, and liberation because of their ability to take flight high up in the heavens, moderators between mortals and the divine to bring prophecies and messages of guidance from above.

There are also many Celtic legends telling how druids could shape-shift into creatures that bore feathers and could transcend high up in the sky. One of the most widely known are of Ceridwen, the witch that could turn into a hawk, and Taliesin, a wizard and companion of King Arthur, who could also turn into a bird.

In *mythology more generally* birds are the inspiration for dragons, those fabled flying creatures, and doves, eagles, and phoenixes appear and reappear in religious sculpture and pictography, icons, calligraphy, and pictogram manuscripts. There are in fact countless mythical birds in legend and folklore – too many to elaborate here – known in many eras and cultures around the world, now too in film and fantasy, among them the Russian storm-driving wind-spirit alkonest, the sirin from Persia, symbol of peace and paradise, the wildrock of Arabian legend and beyond, and of course the wondrous fire-filled phoenix of many lands, symbol of hope, renewal and the continuity of the soul.

In Christian iconography it is the dove, the mystic sign not only of peace but of the Holy Spirit, the third member of the Trinity.

And we must not omit magpies, proverbial for collecting shiny objects, and the jackdaw with its scientific name *corvus monedula* which means "money crow". Early Christian lore stated that corvids were originally white but turned black while mourning the Crucifixion, excepting the magpie which was too busy pilfering so remained partly white!

Crows and other corvids are also widely seen as omens of ill-luck or death, and the magpie is still a herald of fortune ("One for sorrow, Two for joy…"). This derives from their tendency to scavenge carrion and devour the slain on battlefields: "the raven screamed aloft, black and greedy for corpses", wrote one Anglo-Saxon poet.

Odin with his ravens (Ranveig)

The crow and raven are also traditionally considered wise – they are in fact among the most intelligent birds – as being connected to the otherworld and the divine laws of harmony. In keeping with this, the Scandinavian god Odin had two ravens, Huginn and Muninn ("thought and memory") who told him every secret seen or whispered in every part of the world. The ancestral Maratha spirits in India resided in crows; in Egypt a pair of crows symbolised *conjugal felicity;* and in the Aboriginal cultures of Australia and in many North American native myths a Raven appears as a dual-natured Trickster and Creator God, credited with bringing fire, light, sexuality, song, dance and life itself to humankind.

In Celtic lore, the raven belonged to the Welsh hero-king Bran ("raven") supposedly buried under the Tower of London. A ceremonial Raven Master still keeps watch over the birds of the Tower and folklore has it that if they ever leave, the kingdom will fall. Crows and ravens have, as we have seen, also long been considered soul-guides, carrying the dead into the next world as well as able to return as souls to this world. A folk tradition states that King Arthur will return as a raven, and even into the twentieth century people were warned not to harm a raven – "it might be Arthur". This was the basis of the 1994 folklore-fuelled film "The Crow", starring Brandon Lee (his name incidentally means "crow") who was accidentally killed on set during the filming.

Ravens at the Tower of London

Birds have been creatures of the mythic imagination since the very earliest times. Various birds, from eagles to starlings, serve as messengers to the gods in stories the world over, carrying blessings to humankind and prayers up to the heavens. They lead shamans into the Spirit World and dead souls to the Realm Beyond; they follow heroes on quests, uncover secrets, give warning and shrewd council.

The magical snow-white healing caladrius of Roman mythology

The movements, cries and migratory patterns of birds have also been seen as oracles, seriously treated as such in classical times. In Celtic lands, ravens were domesticated as divinatory birds, and eagles, geese and the humble wren also had prophetic *powers*. Odin's two ravens flew through the world each dawn, then perched on his shoulder to whisper news into his ears. A dove with the power of human speech sat in the branches of the sacred oak grove at Zeus's oracle at Dodona; a woodpecker was the oracular bird in groves sacred to Mars.

According to various Siberian peoples, the eagle was the first shaman, sent to humankind by the gods to heal sickness and suffering. Frustrated that human beings could not understand its speech or ways, the bird mated with a human woman; all shamans are descended from their child. In a mystic cloak of bird feathers, the shaman chants, drums and prays him – or herself into a trance. The soul takes flight, soaring into the spirit world beyond our everyday perception.

A swan-maiden was the mother of Cuchulain, hero of Ireland's Ulster cycle, and thus the warrior had a geas (taboo) against killing these sacred birds. In "The Children of Lir", one of the Three Great Sorrows of Irish mythology, the four children of the lord of the sea are transformed into wild swans by the magic of a jealous step-mother. The curse was finally ended but for centuries Irish people would not harm a swan because of this.

It is still widely believed – and enshrined in one of the most beautiful of madrigals – that a swan sings only *once* (its "swan song") in the moments before it dies.

Crows and ravens are omnipresent in myth and folklore. The crow, commonly portrayed as a trickster or thief, was an ominous portent – and yet crows were also sacred to Apollo in Graeco–Roman myth; to Varuna, guardian of the sacred order in Vedic myth; and to Amaterasu Omikami, the sun-goddess of old Japan.

The crane too can is sometimes associated with death, one of the shapes assumed by the King of the Celtic underworld, and to the druids was a portent of treachery and *evil*, *yet* elsewhere it was sacred to and a messenger of the spring. In Japan the crane is now a symbol of peace and the white cranes in Chinese lore inhabited the Isles of the Blest. In some cultures a *crane guide*s the hero on his adventures; and tales about cranes who marry human men can be found throughout the far East.

The wren is another "fairy bird". It was sacred to Celtic druids and a portent of fairy encounters. It was known as the king of the birds, explained in story that the birds held a parliament and decided that whoever could fly the highest and fastest would be crowned king. The eagle easily outdistanced the others, but the clever wren hid under its wing until the eagle faltered – then the wren jumped out and flew higher.

The dove is precious in many traditions, symbolising light, healing, and the transition from one state of existence to the next. It is the subject of many legends as well standing fir peace and representing the third presence – the spirit – in the Christian Trinity.

In many ancient traditions geese are holy, protected, birds. The great Nile Goose was said to have created the world by laying the cosmic egg from which the sun was hatched, and the goose was sacred to Isis, Osiris, Horus, *Hera,* and Aphrodite. In India, a goose – a solar symbol – drew the chariot of Vishnu, representing learning and eloquence. Caesar tells us that geese were sacred in Britain, and thus forbidden as food – a custom still existent in certain Gaelic areas today. Goose-girls, talking geese, and the goose who lays golden eggs are all standard ingredients in the folk tales ("Mother Goose" tales) of Europe.

The stork is another goddess *bird*, sacred to nursing mothers, which may be why it appears in folklore carrying newborn babies to earth.

The pelican is symbolic of women's faith, sacrifice, and maternal devotion, due to the belief that it feeds its young on the blood of its own breast.

Kites and gulls are the souls of dead fisherman returned to haunt the shores, The lark, the linnet, the robin, the loonbird have their own takes, winging their way between heaven and earth in sacred stories, folktales, fairy tales, old rhymes and folkways from around the globe.

The following prayer comes from the Highlands of Scotland, recorded (in Gaelic) more than one hundred years ago:

Power of raven be yours,
Power of eagle be yours,
Power of the Fiann.
Power of storm be yours,
Power of moon be yours,
Power of sun.
Power of sea be yours,
Power of land be yours,
Power of heaven.

Goodness of sea be yours,
Goodness of earth be yours,
Goodness of heaven.
Each day be joyous to you,
No day be grievous to you,
Honor and compassion.
Love of each face be yours,
Death on pillow be yours,
And God be with you.

Birds in literature verse and proverb

Feeding on this deep background of myth and fable, birds are everywhere in verbal art. One story is this:

> *A long time ago, after the last world had been destroyed and a new one created, the People were living in harmony with all of the other creatures of the earth and being thankful for what they had. Slowly but surely they started to drift away again, and the Creator of All Things looked down with sorrow that this cycle would again be repeated. It was decided that on the next day at sunrise the world would again be renewed.*
>
> *Now the eagle is the one who flies highest and sees farthest, and the eagle knew there were still those who were celebrated the old ways, the Ways of Harmony. The next morning, before dawn the eagle left the perch and flew over the land, seeing the puffs of smoke here and there from those who were making offerings of thanksgiving and prayers for others. Then the eagle began circling, higher and higher, higher than ever before, until finally the eagle came to the ear of the Creator.*
>
> *"Stop! You must not do this!" cried the eagle, and the Creator reached out a hand and held back the sun from rising. The Creator knew that the eagle had wisdom and so paused to hear the eagle's argument. The eagle asked the Creator to look, and to truly See those who were still celebrating the Way of Being, those who were celebrating the Old Ways, and in so doing, it was decided on that day that as long as there was still one person left who was still doing his/her best to live in harmony with the earth, to celebrate Sacred Mother Life, that the world would be spared.*
>
> *And so, every morning the eagle soars over the land to look for those who are still living in thankfulness, and every morning, just before dawn, the Creator reaches out a hand to hold back the sun for a moment, waiting for the eagle's report.*

A moral for how we should conduct our days?

And in other literature? Jackdaws are active and individual protagonists in countless literary works. There is Richard Harris Barham's witty poem about a Cardinal's bird, *The Jackdaw of Rheims*, Walter Scott's *Redgauntlet,* the swan in E.B. White's, a gull in *Jonathan Livingston Seagull*, the fantasy dodo *in Alice in Wonderland*. The raven *Grip* is a key character in Dickens' *Barnaby Rudge,* inspiring *Edgar Allan Poe*'s most famous poem, *The Raven* (many others are listed in https://tinyurl.com/44h235bm and https://tinyurl.com/2z7nzm5r).

Hitchcock's film *The Birds* shows feathered fiends pecking out eyes and terrorising a California town. Pterodactyls too come in novels, films and video games, pictured as creatures with an elongated head crest and large wings in *J. R. R. Tolkien*'s Middle-earth legendarium and the *novel The Nazgûl,* where the nine Black Riders rode *Pterodactyl* – like flying monsters.

And in classical times Aristophanes famous comedy *The Birds* was, as he doubtless intended, interpreted – and still is – as an incisive commentary on human ways and character, and then there are the birds of nursery rhymes – remember "Sing a sing of sixpence … Four and twenty blackbirds…" – children's books (well do I remember) and characters in comics.

Birds have always attracted poets. Among the many bird poems here are a handful of all-time favourites:

The first, from nearly a millennium ago, is a debate between an owl and a nightingale about their respective, very differing, qualities – birds as so often and so wisely (hence this book) imaging human lives and living.

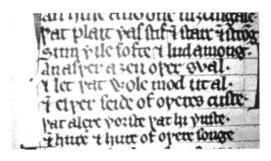

"The owl and the nightingale", first stanza, twelfth century, English

The Phoenix and the Turtle

Let the bird of loudest lay
On the sole Arabian tree
Herald sad and trumpet be,
To whose sound chaste wings obey.
But thou shrieking harbinger,
Foul precurrer of the fiend,
Augur of the fever's end,
To this troop come thou not near.
From this session interdict
Every fowl of tyrant wing,
Save the eagle, feather'd king;
Keep the obsequy so strict …   **William Shakespeare**

This has been called the first metaphysical poem, and takes as its focus the two birds, the mythical phoenix (famed for being able to rise from the ashes of its own funeral pyre) and the turtledove (associated with love).

To a Skylark

Hail to thee, blithe Spirit!
Bird thou never wert,
That from Heaven, or near it,
Pourest thy full heart
In profuse strains of unpremeditated art.
Higher still and higher
From the earth thou springest
Like a cloud of fire;
The blue deep thou wingest,
And singing still dost soar, and soaring ever singest   **Percy Shelley**

The Yellowhammer's Nest

Just by the wooden brig a bird flew up,
Frit by the cowboy as he scrambled down
To reach the misty dewberry – let us stoop
And seek its nest – the brook we need not dread,
'Tis scarcely deep enough a bee to drown,
So it sings harmless o'er its pebbly bed
– Ay here it is, stuck close beside the bank
Beneath the bunch of grass that spindles rank
Its husk seeds tall and high – 'tis rudely planned
Of bleachèd stubbles and the withered fare
That last year's harvest left upon the land,
Lined thinly with the horse's sable hair ...   **John Clare**

Ode to a Nightingale

Thou wast not born for death, immortal Bird!
No hungry generations tread thee down;
The voice I hear this passing night was heard
In ancient days by emperor and clown:
Perhaps the self-same song that found a path
Through the sad heart of Ruth, when, sick for home,
She stood in tears amid the alien corn;
The same that oft-times hath
Charm'd magic casements, opening on the foam
Of perilous seas, in faery lands forlorn ...   **John Keats**

"Hope" is the thing with feathers

"Hope" is the thing with feathers –
That perches in the soul –
And sings the tune without the words –
And never stops – at all ...

Emily Dickinson

The Windhover (opening)

I caught this morning morning's minion, kingdom
Of daylight's dauphin, dapple-dawn-drawn Falcon, in his riding
Of the rolling level underneath him steady air, and striding
High there, how he rung upon the rein of a wimpling wing
In his ecstasy! then off, off forth on swing,
As a skate's heel sweeps smooth on a bow-bend: the hurl and gliding
Rebuffed the big wind. My heart in hiding
Stirred for a bird, – the achieve of, the mastery of the thing!

Gerald Manley Hopkins

King of Carrion

His palace is of skulls.
His crown is the last splinters
Of the vessel of life.
His throne is the scaffold of bones, the hanged thing's
Rack and final stretcher.
His robe is the black of the last blood.
His kingdom is empty–
The empty world, from which the last cry
Flapped hugely, hopelessly away
Into the blindness and dumbness and deafness of the gulf
Returning, shrunk, silent
To reign over silence.

Ted Hughes

Do you?'

Ravens mate for ever
They say, for life
Elephants, deer, and camels,
Man, and wife

They feed their nestlings
Labour of joy
Speak friendship to flockings
Man and boy.

No pause in their love t' each other
No stop to their friendship and love
To their parenting, nesting together
To their flying above there as two.

Oh but ah and again ah, oh my singer,
Is it in you to tell me now true
To my question I ask again, ever –
Do you ... ?

Kate Finn

I like best of all Shakespeare's simple

I have heard
The cock, that is the trumpet to the morn,
Doth with his lofty and shrill-sounding throat
Awake the god of day.

Shakespeare
From the opening scene
of Hamlet

By José Maria de Souza Moura Girão (1840-1916) – Palácio do Correio Velho

And you have no doubt, like me, come across, perhaps used, some of the innumerable proverbs and sayings calling on the behaviour or appearance of birds to comment on and inform our human ways.

A bird does not sing because it has an answer. It sings because it has a song.

The early bird catches the worm, but it is the early worm that gets caught.

A bird in the hand is worth two in the bush.

Birds of a feather flock together.

A bird never flew on one wing.

God loved the birds and invented trees, humans loved the birds and cut down the forests.

A fine cage won't feed a bird.

One swallow does not make a summer.

If it walks like a duck, quacks like a duck, looks like a duck, it is a duck.

Birds in their little nest agree.

Feather your own nest.

As proud as a peacock.

The arrow strikes one bird down, but the flock remains.

I like this one:

If I had to choose a favourite:

I would rather have birds than airplanes.

Charles Lindbergh

Or, longer, but equally to the bird-human point.

Edward Hersey Richards

A wise old owl sat on an oak;
The more he saw the less he spoke;
The less he spoke the more he heard;
Why aren't we like that wise old bird?

Birds, souls and spirits

It is striking that the symbolism and thinking of so many cultures seems to imply a close affinity between humans and birds.

In *trans*migration traditions it is between birds and humans that the transition is most often envisaged: between species that are if not equivalent, even at root identical, *at* the least the most closely related. And it is no coincidence that in myth and art the original *language* on earth was that of birds.

Winged words flying as birds through the Tower of Babel (detail from The Garden of Earthly Delights by Hieronymous Bosch

*In the story i*t was only with the arrogance of the Tower of Babel that the speech of human-kind, once words flying free as birds, became divided and pinned down into our *mortal* languages.

It is notable that, as we have seen, birds are in so many religious traditions regarded as *link*s between the spiritual and earthly *realm*s of being. They bring us messages, warnings, motivation, solace, guide us forward on our spiritual journey, know both past and future, and symbolise higher knowledge, freedom, strength, leadership and the ability to soar higher in face of difficulties – a messengers of elevation, enlightenment, and wisdom.

Different cultures have their own ways of honouring these sacred winged beings, and of recognising their importance and spiritual meaning, not seldom connected with the verbal, dramatic and choreographic arts.

For example, the Inuit (Eskimo) connect birds with the spiritually endowed activities of dance and song, placing a loonbird's bill into a child's mouth to make him/her a good singer. Someone who wants to apprentice to a particular shaman presents him with a tent pole on top of which he has tied a gull's wing. The message is clear: he wishes to fly. Close observers of the natural world, they knew well that loonbirds are not just remarkable vocalists but strongly territorial, visibly aggressive, powerful, direct, and very hard to kill, with the ability, like shamans, to influence other-than-human beings and to "fly through the air like a bird [and] go down into the ocean like a fish," as shamans were said to do.

All this, one might say, is just mythology, although with its own depths. All the same, it is hard to imagine that so many generations, so many cultures, so many people of wisdom and insight who have attributed spiritual qualities to birds, and detected and formulated these in their own language and experience, can all have got it totally wrong.

We are them?

Why are *bird*s so often thought of as the closest to, indeed in some kind of deep sense, *identical* with, *humans*?

How can we tell – except perhaps just to say that many generations have felt it?

Birds, so close to humans, come on gravestones as a sign, we take it, of continuity and freedom: *birds* are those who soar on high – *high*, that potent perhaps universal metaphor – where they see things, more clearly, from the perspective of the sky; birds are the symbols of free flight, of courage, wisdom, endurance; birds are our messengers from heaven and proverbs ostensibly about birds can equally be read as comments on our human selves. Either in general or, in varying traditions, as specific birds, they are the spirits that are in some sense near-identical with ourselves whether as totems, guides or souls, who show us not just wisdom, but somehow our own ways, ourselves.

There is perhaps no need to repeat the examples given earlier but it is worth noting how clearly this aspect comes through in Steven Feld's work with the Kaluli people, *Sound and Sentiment: Birds, Weeping, Poetics and Song in Kaluli Expression*. Living as they do in close proximity to birds in the rain forests in Papua New Guinea, Kaluli speakers both every day and in ritual, literally and metaphorically, seem to see a kind of deep identification and parallelism between themselves and birds. In ritual dance the bird-like dancer flashes from being seen as a bird to being a man and back again, till finally the two merge and we feel what has been two as fundamentally one.

Birds and humans, humans and birds

So where are we now? First, the balance of our mutual relations: who helps most, who hurts? Humans help birds in many ways – well some do, trying, and in a variety of ways.

They put out bird feed – precious resource in winter conditions – provide nesting boxes and bird baths where birds can refresh themselves and drink, break the ice in winter, rescue and care for injured or lost birds, provide refuge centres on migration flyways, try to help threatened species by protected breeding spots and zoological gardens, set up and guard bird sanctuaries. They love and care for and make friends with their caged pet birds. All in all, birds have long featured in human culture as objects of admiration and beauty and, especially the corvids and parrots, as human companions, assistants and domesticated friends.

There are regional, national and international bodies dedicated to the protection, valuing and greater understanding of birds and (some) laws preventing the worst forms of exploitation.

Pond where my granddaughter and I so often threw food for the ducks

Along with similar organisations in many countries, the British Trust for Ornithology (www.bto.org), to take just one example, communicates knowledge and expertise to increase the respect for birds, and champions impartial science by exploring the most pressing questions about birds through their *scientific research.*

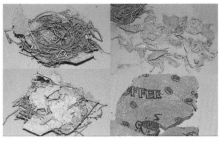

There are less deliberate ways too. We happen to produce and perform the wild rhythmic music that some birds seem to listen to and enjoy and sometimes mimic or dance to. Humans plant orchards and forests, produce materials that can be used for building nests (where even plastics can be made use of) or decorating display stages, for sowing and tending the grain and fruit crops that birds love, in making buildings and hedges where birds can nest. Agriculture and gardening turn up the soil to reveal the worms that birds seek and make them an easier prey – many of us can still recall the flocks that followed the ploughman. or the robin watchfully hanging around as you dig the garden.

And then from the other side, we humans benefit so much from birds. There is the delight we get from the visual beauty of their colours, shapes and flight, from their companionship both wild and captive, from their inspiration for art, for singers, literature and music, feathers for human adornment, and as models for flight, building and weaving, their place in nature'*s loveliness.*

They at times grant us their companionship too, either informally in the wild where they can make friends even slow us a little, at their wish, to be involved in their language and their lives, or as companion animals and pets interacting with and advising us, or as domesticated animals in rough farmsteads through the centuries, arguably with mutual benefits, as geese were for centuries acting as the most vocal and vigilant of watchmen.

In addition, to human but not avian advantage, they have always provided an important part of our nutrition: their flesh from both domesticated and from wild birds but also most importantly from their eggs, a major part of the human diet from away back, and not just from domesticated hens. It is an outstandingly nutritious part too – a single egg is said to contain all the nutritional goodness of a whole chicken.

And then there are the specific events where birds have come to the aid of humans. There were the "miracle sea gulls" of 1848 who in Salt Lake Valley saved the crops on which the Mormons settlers totally depended. Only their second harvest, essential for their survival, it was attacked by a plague of locusts, but flocks of seagull appeared and miraculously saved the crops by eating thousands of the insects that were devouring everything, and saved the settlement (earlier, too, during their trek to the Great Salt Lake, many of them had been saved by the quail that flew into their camp, providing them with food).

The Salt Lake episode is only one case of the frequent help given by birds in controlling locusts. Certain birds such as storks, crows, kites, rosy starling birds, and peafowls eat locusts, for them a good source of protein. They sit near crops as this is where locusts spend most of their time so it is easy for birds to pick them out one by one.

Not to their liking no doubt but providing occupation or wages for generations of children is the seasonal attempts to scare birds from the growing crops, resulting in cheerful bird chasers' songs like:

> *Ye pigeons and crows, away, away!*
> *Why do you steal my master's tea?*
> *If he should come with his long gun,*
> *You must fly and I must run.*

And then of course, as we well know, birds are a continual source of delight in their appearance, sounds, wisdom, spirituality.

But of course, it's not all good. There is much, very much, on the debit side.Since the 17th century 130 species have become extinct due to human activity, and hundreds more before then. True there have been attempts to protect them, but as forest are cut down, marshlands drained, and wild places built over, human actions currently threaten 1,200 or more bird species with extinction. Humans plunder eggs and nests, sometimes perhaps with the best of intentions but the birds and eggs are dead nevertheless.

Humans have always hunted birds for food. So of course, have birds of prey. But to this, humans now add shooting and *trapping* just for sport and go out of their way to *preserve* "game" birds dedicated to the same fate. Birds are domesticated not just for love but for profit and sale, kept in sometimes horrific conditions for their eggs and their meat. Some indeed are reared with care and in cooperation with their human falconry owners trained to engage in their own natural activity of hunting other birds. But might they not prefer to do it freely in their own time and space? The same for pet and laboratory birds however well treated?

Pesticides, pollution, industrial waste, high buildings, light and noise pollution, factory farming and the horrifying system of battery-caged fowl for egg-production have added to the toll. Forests have been cut down, habitats interfered with, sea filled with plastics, fly-stops destroyed.

There are ways the birds fight back too, specially but not exclusively the *larger birds*.

Swans are all known for being prepared to pull down and drown dogs near their piece of waters or even break an arm of someone they think is coming too close to their nest. An angry bird getting in your hair can be terrifying and actively on the attack, and with the bird memory for faces will not be easily given up.

Birds are at their most aggressive in spring, protecting their nests and the ground beneath since baby birds learn to fly by jumping from the nest. Some birds are specially likely to attack (not necessarily the largest): starlings are one – they look so small and harmless, but ...

Attacks by gulls are common – they swoop down aggressively on family groups to snatch picnic titbits. Canada geese also have a long history of attacking humans and above all, by the intensely territorial America crows, who are liable to dive and strike you not just once, but repetitively and what is more notify their flock mates about your memorised face.

Magpies can be particularly aggressive. It is true that they only attack people for a few weeks during the nesting season, mainly, and understandably, when the chicks have just left the nest and are being protected by their parents. But even this short period can be dangerous enough to humans. Over a hundred children at a school in Australia had their faces cut open by an attacking magpie, and a subsequent survey of 5000 people revealed that 96% of men and 75% of women had been victims of a magpie attack at some time in their lives. There are now public warnings in susceptible areas.

It seems that with greater human encroachment on birds' habitats bird attacks are increasing. They may start with a sudden whack on the back of the head, a fierce fiercely opened claws, or a relentlessly pecking beak. This can be enough to drive people to abandon their once tranquil walks or cycle rides, change their routes, wear protective headgear or furiously wave arms above their heads as they jog, leaving the birds free to enjoy *their* once tranquil habits and nesting sites on which humans had been encroaching. An avian victory – the more so that males benefit from attacking people; they generally don't hurt themselves and it looks great to the females that they have chased these big predators away!

Birds may mostly be small compared to humans and fight back only in little ways, but, specially when they act in concert, there have ways to keep their end up – the balance is not *always* in the humans' favour.

Yes, today's *dinosaurs*, the birds, are physically very different from us *human*s. While our mammal relatives were busy growing, birds were busy shrinking. While our ancestors were learning to walk on two feet, theirs were perfecting lightness and flight – a development, we used to think, that severely limited their brain size and cognitive skill (could creatures whose brains are smaller than ours and so different possibly be clever?).

Professor Murray Shanahan of the Department of Computing at Imperial College London, elaborates: "Birds have been evolving separately from mammals for around 300 million years, so it is hardly surprising that under a microscope the brain of a bird looks quite different from a mammal. Yet, birds have been shown to be remarkably intelligent in a similar way to mammals such as humans and monkeys."

His team analysed 34 studies of the anatomy of the pigeon brain, a typical one for a bird. They focussed on areas called 'hub nodes', the regions of the brain that firm the major centres for processing information and for high level cognition. In particular, they looked at the hippocampus, which is important for navigation and long-term memory in both birds and mammals. They found that these hub nodes had very dense connections to other parts of the brain in both kinds of animal, suggesting they function in a similar way. They also compared the prefrontal cortex in mammals, which is important for complex thought such as decision making. They discovered that despite these hub nodes having evolved differently, the way they are wired up within the brain looks similar.

So yes, in some ways we are now very different. But to return to our central question – *are* birds *so* very different from us in character, and actions? In essentials?

Consider the evidence we now have, summarised in the chapters above. How does it accord with our accepted hominid characteristics?

Locomotion – homo bipedalis

Bipedalism: are there any parallels here?

Well, birds too ultimately developed out of tetrapods (four-footed) creatures, but their forelimbs instead of, as with humans, evolving into tool-using arms and hands, became wings. We are very different from each other by now in both anatomy and function from ours, and yet with the same foundation and origin..

With their hopping, walking, running and paddling feet, birds are certainly, like us, bipedal. Both humans and birds – four-limbed like other mammals and dinosaurs – also, additionally, put their upper limbs to good use, in the one case as wings, in the other as manipulating hands, but nothing there that undermines the essentially two-legged gait.

No great contrast there.

The extra dimension of different usage of the forelimbs does make quite a difference however and one that is worth noting. If birds fall short of humans in the manipulation of tools then the opposite is true in respect of flight – birds' ability to move through the air by the action of their own bodies. There are indeed exceptions and some birds (still bipedal) seldom or never fly, in general for birds the ability to fly is a typical and fine avian characteristic, the opposite of how we humans are.

So in that respect quite a difference.

Tool using – homo faber et habilis

On the face of it this is a huge difference. Even with their much longer evolutionary history birds have never developed a fingered human-like hand and opposable thumb that have made resource manipulation and sophisticated technology such a striking human achievement – the sharpest, it seems, of the contrasts between birds and humans.

So yes, in the number and diversity of the tools they use or construct birds are very different from us. But in essentials, rather than detail, are they really so different? Just as we do, they select and use the tools that work for their needs and desires – what more should they want? And, how important is the difference really? In terms of desired achievements and aims?

Perhaps there is an argument for giving comparable credit to the arguably equally intelligent use and creation of tools and manipulation of resources by birds for their own purposes?

So – hugely different, yes, but we can still debate the import of the differences.

Social beings – homo socialis

Both birds and humans are notably social beings (yes of course there are individual exceptions but they are just that – exceptions).

Birds are arguably even more sociable than humans. From birth and even before they most often live-in groups, they learn together, live together, fly together, migrate together. They normally pair together at least for a season – socially though not necessarily sexually monogamous (the male may well not have fathered all of the chicks he is devotedly caring for) and is sometimes a pairing lasting for life. preceded by flamboyant courting displays (though, as with humans, one may sometimes stray).

Parenting: unlike the majority of mammals both bird parents take a direct and hands-on responsibility for caring for, teaching, and bringing up their young.

So, much the same apart from the detailed contexts.

Migrating, adventuring, navigating – homo migrans et navigans

Starting from (we now think) South Africa, humans went on in prehistoric times to people the globe. More recently but still going back hundreds or thousands of years, they ventured in out open boats across the oceans to inhabit new lands, and found their way in sailing ships across the world – impressive navigation, adventuring, courage. Is there any way birds can match this?

Yes and no – birds do it differently and arguably even more impressively. There is a possible link, as bird migrations may well have provided the models and guides for human venturing.

Speaking, planning, thinking

Both birds and humans are constant communicators, in both cases predominantly but not exclusively by vocal means. And birds, some birds at any rate, are planners, thinkers, manipulators, problem solvers par excellence, amazing learners and teachers in and from new situations, highly intelligent. As are humans.

The avian results may at first have seemed startling. As humans we don't really think that, psychologically, birds are capable of the same mental tasks that other mammals are, above all hominids. But birds too, some at least, arguably have cognitive abilities similar to those of our close relatives, in some cases even exceeding them. Some birds are tool-makers, count, sew and weave, and some have learned elements of the language of a very different species (ourselves). Some are capable of empathy, altruism, love, and appear to mourn, or at least acknowledge, their dead, just as we do. Some birds too have been shown to possess skills such as complex social reasoning, an ability to problem solve and, with some, the capability to craft complex tools.

It seems there may be a neurological basis and explanation for this. At any ratewe we are now increasingly aware of some birds' ability for planning and though-out puzzle solving, and the deliberate self-conscious use of language, And, then there seems to be an – unexpected – ability to generalise and to predict from specific experienced instances, in other words to conceptualise.

So, both birds and humans – not all, but many – would appear have foresight for the future, have good memories and strategies for planning, and both, it seems, have a degree of self-awareness, of identity and, varying of course with the individual and (for birds) with the species, a capacity for adapting.

In all this, learning, both from own experience and from others, and adapting appropriately would seems to be key in birds' survival – as it is, too, for humans.

Artistry and play – homo ludens

On both sides, communication and action, while put to good and necessary use, are not solely utilitarian but also, it seems, for play (where did humans first get the idea of playing with a ball?) and for delight. So too for (in both cases) aesthetic appreciation of visual display, of creative innovation, dance, and (where did humans pick up this magnificent habit) for the wonderfully colourful proud show-off displays of courtship.

And then there is music. As an ethnomusicologist, I am myself persuaded that though there is certainly some exchange from both sides, human music owes both its ultimate origin and much of its shaping to birdsong, and regard this as arguably the greatest of the many gifts that birds have given us.

Rulers of the world – homo regnans

Perhaps, perhaps not. It is a question.

But in these days of climate change, of an increasing sensitivity to ecology, and of the rise of the green movement, it seems that human assumptions of sovereignty over the earth and disregard of its other creatures, not least of birds, may be suffering something of a setback. Now may be a moment to resume a equal respect for, among other things, the enduring wisdom and value of birds.

The final jury – you – is still out

So –?

What are we to conclude about the respective situations of humans and of birds?

Differences, yes certainly, but not as many or as radical as is often thought, and also some striking similarities. A parallel species indeed, or, looked at from another perspective, two complementary sets of beings.

For birds too have "culture", something anthropologists and others once thought a purely human trait. They too learn and share new ways which may then, as with humans, if found to be useful and adopted, become the shared tradition of that culture, whether just locally or more widely.

This aspect of culture was well exemplified in the way an experimentally induced innovation led to persistent culture change among wild birds. Two great tits, known to be highly innovated foragers, were caught and taught to open doors to get food. When they were released back into the wild they carried on these techniques which others then copied, and they became embedded as cultural traditions.

Arguably the key thing to emerge from all this, and possibly at first sight the most surprising, is that birds are in general *able and prepared to learn* from observation, from experience and from others, to pass on what they have learnt to others, to adapt to new situations, and to act as members in a shared and specific culture. At the same time, perhaps to our minds counter–intuitively, they have some *appreciation of individual identity*. In all this there is much in common with human cultures.

So each of these two parallel species have learned, are still learning from each other. True, birds have the advantage of many millions more years in which to have learned and developed their arts. But maybe humans too have given something, like new tunes or different tools or new ways of having fun, and it is possible in the future may do still more – birds have certainly shown that when they wish they are very apt to learn. They have heard and repeated back human songs, they have carefully watched and copied humans casting bait on the waters to catch their prey, they have looked at how humans use particular tools and copied them. Always opportunists, they pick up and use new materials made by humans, bits of metal or plastics being only some of the examples they turn to their own purposes as tools or nest material, They are by no means slow to catch on!

But most of all, it seems, it is we humans who have learned and copied.

Flying

Yes of course humans now sometimes travel through the air and need to, but without wings they cannot on their own get very far. Humans after all do not naturally fly, unlike birds who, face it, are dinosaurs with bodies specialised for flight. With millions of years to have developed the complex biomechanics of flight they have served as the models for human endeavours in the air.

Red Arrows – aeroplanes, yes, inspired by the lift and group flying of birds

A flock of domestic pigeons each in a different phase of its flap

For how would humans ever have thought of flying without seeing the flight of birds and emulating it in dreams and reality? where did they find their models of floating above the earth or hovering in the air? of staying aloft or fleeting full speed forward? of formation flying? of swooping to the heavens and staying there? of slowing for safe landing? Where else but from birds?

Or from where else could we have imagined the design of an object intended for flight – the long smooth low-air-resistant body designed for forward flying, the invaluable heavy contents behind, the spread wings, the narrow pointing head, the balancing tail, forward thrust, the legs / undercarriage to be folded and retracted once aloft?

And then the actual flying – not just some single straightforward once-and-for-all process, but a complex of bio-mechanical principles which it was for human aero-engineers to figure out.

Navigating and exploring

With birds' long developed flyways and navigating ability, it is no longer such a puzzle that in earlier times, before modern navigation aids, *human* animals too were inspired to emulate and follow the avian routes, and venture across the seas for thousands of miles to Aotearoa (New Zealand) and other islands in the remote *Pacific.*

Social beings

It is likely that as with some other mammals, humans have been social animals from the start but some of the detailed ways in which they exhibit this we're likely copied or inspired birds, who have after been around, and learning for so much longer than we have. We could mention for example coordinated joint action for hunting, attack, defence, building, or the teamwork of bi-parenting.

Music

And it is surely from birds that we have learned to hear the beauty and art of music and ventured to try it ourselves. Perhaps the same is true of dancing and and a feeling for rhythm (check out the amazing utube videos of cockatoos' marvellous dancing) and of play generally.

Rulers of the world and all that is and was and will be in it

Maybe – but is it perhaps time for us to see ourselves, we humans, less as rulers than as joint guardians? jointly with all creatures around us indeed but arguably above all with our avian partners, parallel beings through millions of years, the birds?

Generally

As Noah Strycker, who knows well what he is talking about, sums it up: *"In almost any realm of bird behaviour – reproduction, populations, movements, daily rhythms, communication, navigation, intelligence, and so on – there are deep and meaningful parallels with our own".*

But, finally, we should at the same time not overlook the unique arts of each: of birds their flight, of such infinite material and symbolic worth; and for humans that great gift, let us never minimise it and *not* the property of birds, of complex, verbalised, language, and the many means for capturing and preserving it.

It is a gift not to be forgotten.

For the earth

It is ours. We, birds and humans, in our interacting lives on earth, share the responsibility for its *care*.

We are perhaps not as wise as birds, they have had many more millions of years of learning than we have. But that means we have had the chance to learn from what they have discovered: to experience the biomechanics of flight; build and plan; see the coils of mud become the superb human achievement of pottery; create and feel the delights of music and song and play; learn the ways across and over the sea; and then, now, to reflect how birds have lived and learned and adapted through the earth's many climate changes over the countless years of earth's life. So why not we humans likewise?

Pietà *– depicts the body of Jesus on the lap of his caring mother Mary after the Crucifixion*

We, birds and humans, *are* indeed two, communicating, species in more ways than is usually recognised. To a degree we learn from and understand each other. We share the sowing and reaping of fruits. We are both social beings and learn from and copy each other's music and ways of flying and navigation. We share a sense of beauty, of joy, and of sorrow.

We are interacting social animals and we guard but do not possess this earth in which we live, perhaps each with still much to learn and far to go.

We humans have of the art of verbal language, the wisdom of proverb and philosophy, the beauty of poetry. Where in birds can we find a Shakespeare, a William Blake, a Homer, a Rumi? No particular credit to us, a gift – just, it is there.

But the beauty and speed of flight, the regularity of care and affection, the curiosity and intellect, the brilliance of migrating flocks – that is for us to admire in birds.

Arguably birds, older, have in some ways the advantage over us humans, but for now, two parallel species, do we not share the responsibility and care for our beautiful planet?

Birds from long time past have inhabited and guarded the earth, and now we, with our own qualities too, are joining them. Do we, ourselves, have something precious, ourselves, to offer?

But, however that may be, here we are, two great branches of living beings, not identical but close, parallel, to a degree independent, to a degree interacting, with much in common but each with our own uniquenesses and of equal worth. It is given to us both, surely, to cherish and care for our beautiful earth.

It is for us, jointly, to take on and recognise that precious responsibility. *We* share its custody.

May we indeed do *so*.

The Blue Marble *is an image of Earth taken on December 7, 1972, by the Apollo 17 crew Harrison Schmitt and Ron Evans from a distance of about 29,000 kilometers (18,000 miles) from the planet's surface*

Questions for reflection, discussion or debate

What most surprised you (and your friends) in this book?

Do you know anyone who in any way talks with birds?

    If so what do they say about it and do you believe them?

How many birds can you and / or your friends and family identify?

    And their songs or calls?

    And does it matter?

How far, in your opinion, do humans communicate in the same way(s) as birds?

    Why do you think that?

In your opinion are humans the rulers of the world, or ought they to be?

    Why or why not?

Do you think it makes sense to regard birds as fellow custodians of the earth?

    Why or why not?

What single topic about birds would you most like to see research on in the future?

    Why?

You might also like

http://www.youtube.com/watch?v=vqqwb3Zcy1U gangnam style parrot dance/

https://corvidresearch.blog/2015/03/16/crow-curiosities-do-crows-play-and-why/

J. Ackerman, *The Genius of Birds,* 2016.

Theodore Xenophon Barber, *The Human Nature of Birds: A Scientific Discovery with Startling Implications,* 1994.

Yuval Noah Harari, *Sapiens: A Brief History of Humankind,* 2015.

Irene Pepperbe, *The Alex studies: cognitive and communicative abilities of grey parrots,* 1999.

References

A complete set of sources for this book may be found at: www.ruthhfinnegan.com/birds-and-humans-references

Ackerman, J., The Genius of Birds, 2016.

Adam Fishbein, February 2, 2018 (Scientific American).

Andrew M. Berdahl et al. 'Collective animal navigation and migratory culture: from theoretical models to empirical evidence' (review article), Philosophical Transactions of the Royal Society B Biological Sciences, 26 March 2018. https://royalsocietypublishing.org/

Barber, Theodore Xenophon, The Human Nature of Birds: A Scientific Discovery with Startling Implications, 1994.

Barnard, Alan, Hunter–Gatherers, What We Can Learn from Them, 2020.

Beckers, Gabriël J. L. et al. "A bird's eye view of human language evolution", Front. Evol. Neurosci., 13 April 2012.

Beecher, M. D. & Brenowitz, E. A. "Functional aspects of song learning in songbirds".

Birds in Legend, Fable and Folklore by E. Ingersoll and Tari Warwick, 2020.

Birds use language like humans joining calls together to form sentences, The Daily Telegraph, 2015, Mar 8.

Boswall, J. (1998). "Answering the calls of nature: human mimicry of avian voice", Transactions of Leicester Literary and Philosophical Society. 92: 10-11.

Bottjer, S. W. & Johnson, F. Circuits, hormones, and learning: vocal behavior in songbirds. Journal of Neurobiology 33, 1997.

Brainard, M. S. & Doupe, A. J. What songbirds teach us about learning. Nature 417, 2002.

Brenowitz, E. A. et al. An intro. to birdsong and the avian song system. Journal of Neurobiology 33, 1997.

C. R. Raby et al. "Facebook". Nature, 2007, 445 (7130).

Catchpole, C. K. & Slater, P. J. B. Bird song: Biological Themes and Variations, 2008.

David Attenborough, The Life of Birds, 1998.

David E. Alexander, Nature's Flyers: Birds, Insects, and the Biomechanics of Flight. 2002.

David Rothenberg, Why birds sing, 2005.

Garth C Clifford, Bird Symbolism & Meaning (+Totem, Spirit & Omens), 2021, https://www.worldbirds.org/bird-symbolism/

Guss, David M., ed, The Language of the Birds, 1986.

Haesler, S. et al. "Incomplete and inaccurate vocal imitation after knockdown of FoxP2 in songbird basal ganglia nucleus area X", PLoS Biology 5, 2007.

Harari, Yuval Noah, Homo deus. A, A Brief History of Tomorrow, 2017.

Harari, Yuval Noah, Sapiens. A Brief History of Humankind, 2015.

Hayward, Guy "How do singers and other groups synchronise to form gcommunities?" in Ruth Finnegan, ed., Entrancement, Consciousness in Dreaming, Music and the World, 2019.

Hollis Taylor, Is Birdsong Music? 2017.

Huxley, T.H. (1876): Lectures on Evolution. New York Tribune. Extra 36, Collected Essays IV, https://mathcs.clarku.edu/huxley/CE4/LecEvol.html

Irene Pepperberg (2006). "Grey parrot numerical competence: a review". Animal Cognition. 9 (4).

Irene Pepperberg, 1999 The Alex studies: cognitive and communicative abilities of Grey parrots, 1999.

Jeffrey Sward, "Cuckoo and Other Bird Sounds Used in Classical Music", 2016 (Wikipedia).

Konishi, M. The role of auditory feedback in the control of vocalization in the white-crowned sparrow. Zeitschrift fur Tierpsychologie 22, 1965.

Konrad Lorenz, King Solomon's Ring, 2002.

Laudanum, Nooshin, (1998). "The Song of the Nightingale: Processes of Improvisation in Dastgāh Segāh (Iranian Classical Music)", British Journal of Ethnomusicology, 1998,.7

Low, Chris, "Birds and Khoesān, linking spirits and healing with day-to-day life", 2011 (https://www.jstor.org/stable/41485278

Luis Felipe Baptista and Robin A. Keister, "Why Birdsong is Sometimes Like Music". Perspectives in Biology and Medicine, 2005, 48, 3.

MacDougall-Shackleton, S. A. "Sexual selection and the evolution of song repertoires." In Current Ornithology, vol. 14, eds. V. J. Nolan, E. D. Ketterson, & C. F. Thompson (New York, NY: Plenum Press, 1997.

MacDougall-Shackleton, S. A. et al. "Nonlocal male mountain white-crowned sparrows have lower paternity and higher parasite loads than males singing local dialect", Behavioral Ecology 13, 2002.

Mâche, François-Bernard (1993) Music, Myth and Nature, or The Dolphins of Arion.

Marker, Peter; Hans Willem Slabbekoorn (2004). Nature's music: the science of birdsong.

Marler, P. A comparative approach to vocal learning: song development in white-crowned sparrows. Journal of Comparative & Physiological Psychology 71, 1970.

Marler, Peter; Hans Willem Slabbekoorn, Nature's music: the science of birdsong, 2004.

Maynard Smith, John and David Harper, D. Animal Signals, 2004.

Maynard Smith, John, "Birds as aeroplanes", New Biology 1954, 14.

McSherry, David (18 May 2014). "Nightingale & Violin Duet – 90 Years Since 1st Outside Broadcast". University of Lincoln.

Michael Silvers, "Attending to the Nightingale: on a Multispecies Ethnomusicology". Ethnomusicology 2020 64 (2)..

Mike Hansell (2000). Bird Nests and Construction Behaviour, 2000.

Mooney, R. "Neurobiology of song learning", Current Opinion in Neurobiology 19, 2009.

Morrison, Lesley, The Healing Wisdom of Birds, 2011.

N.J. Emery and N.S. Clayton "The mentality of crows: convergent evolution of intelligence in corvids and apes". Science 2004, 306 (5703).

Nathan F Putman "Animal navigation: What is truth?" Current Biology 31, 7, 12 April 2021.

Nelson, D. A. & Marler, P. Selection-based learning in bird song development. Proceedings of the National Academy of Sciences USA 91, 1994.

Nettl, Bruno (1987). The radif of Persian music – studies of structure and cultural context.

Nichola S. Clayton et al. "Social cognition by food-caching corvids. The western scrub-jay as a natural psychologist". Phil. Trans. R. Soc. B. 2007, 362 (1480).

Nooshin, Laudan (1998). "The Song of the Nightingale: Processes of Improvisation in Dastgāh Segāh (Iranian Classical Music)". British Journal of Ethnomusicology. 7…

Norell, M & Ellison M (2005). Unearthing the Dragon, The Great Feathered Dinosaur Discovery.

Nozedar, Adele, Secret Language of Birds, 2006.

Padian K (ed.). The Origin of Birds and the Evolution of Flight. Mem. California Acad. Sci 8.

Peter Friederici, "The bird that never forgets", National Wildlife 1 Oct, 2000.

Pradeep Raja Kannaiah | Dreamstime.com. Parrots Cuddling ©

Raby, C. R., Alexis, D. M.; P, Dickinson, A. Clayton, N. S. (2007). "Planning for the future by western scrub–jays". Nature. 445 (7130).

Ravens at the Tower of London © Colin / Wikimedia Commons, CC BY–SA 4.0.

Rebecca Franks (22 February 2016). "Six of the best: pieces inspired by birdsong". Classical-Music.com.

Reid, Chris (2017). "Is birdsong music? Ask the butcherbird". RealTime Arts.

Robert Burton et al. Bird behavior, 1985.

Robert Burton, Bird Flight. Facts on File, 1990.

Rothenberg, David (2005). Why Birds Sing.

Sanga, Imani (2006). "Kumpolo: Aesthetic Appreciation and Cultural Appropriation of Bird Sounds in Tanzania". Folklore. 117 (1).

Shepard Krech III, The Nature and Culture of Birds, https://nationalhumanitiescenter.org/on-the-human/2011/03/nature-and-culture-of-birds/

Silvers, Michael (2020). "Attending to the Nightingale: On a Multispecies Ethnomusicology". Ethnomusicology. 64 (2)

Steven Feld, Sound and Sentiment: Birds, Weeping, Poetics and Song in Kaluli Expression, 1990.

Strycker, Noah, The Magic and Mystery of Birds: The Surprising Lives of Birds and What They Reveal About Being Human, 2014

Suthers, R. (2004). "How birds sing and why it matters". In Marler, P. Slabbekoorn, H. (eds.). Nature's music: The science of birdson.

T. B. Jones and A.C. Kamil, A. C. (1973). "Tool-making and tool-using in the northern blue jay". Science 1973, 180 (4090).

Taylor, Hollis (2017). "Is Birdsong Music?".

The Folklore of Birds by Edward A. Armstrong, 1970.

Thorpe, W. H. "The learning of song patterns by birds, with especial reference to the song of the chaffinch Fringilla coelebs", Ibis 100, 1958.

Toshitaka N. Suzuki, David Wheatcroft and Michael Griesser "Call combinations in birds and the evolution of compositional syntax", Plos Biology, August 15, 2018.

Traykov, Stanislav - Cut out and cropped., CC BY 2.5, https://commons.wikimedia.org/w/index.php?curid=3667082. Pietà (Michelangelo)

Trends in Ecology and Evolution 20, 2005.

W. H. Thorpe, "Antiphonal Singing in Birds as Evidence for Avian Auditory Reaction Time". Nature. 23 February 1963, 197 (4869).

Wada, H. (2010) The Development of Birdsong. Nature Education Knowledge 3, 10.

West, M. J. & King, A. P. Female visual displays affect the development of male song in the cowbird. Nature 334, 1988.

White, S. A. et al. "Singing mice, songbirds, and more: models for FOXP2 function and dysfunction in human speech and language", Journal of Neuroscience, 2006.

Wilford, John Noble (28 March 2016). "Dinosaurs Among Us' Retraces an Evolutionary Path". The New York Times.

Wong, Kate. "How Birds Evolved Their Incredible Diversity". S11

Zina Deretsky, National Science Foundation. Diagram of bone structure.

Photos not otherwise referenced in web sources, by **John Hunt** at www.mapperou.com
Page

9 781739 893781